SAN DIEGO PUBLIC LIBRARY
Point Loma Branch

WITHDRAWN

P9-DXE-882

SMITHSONIAN NATIONAL AIR AND SPACE MUSEUM, WASHINGTON, D.C.
IN ASSOCIATION WITH HARRY N. ABRAMS, INC., PUBLISHERS

CHARLES LINDBERGH AND
THE SPIRIT OF ST. LOUIS

SAN DIEGO PUBLIC LIBRARY
Point Loma Branch

by **DOMINICK A. PISANO** *and* **F. ROBERT VAN DER LINDEN**

FOREWORD BY REEVE LINDBERGH

JUL 1 0 2002

New photography by Eric Long and Mark Avino

EDITORS: Eric Himmel, Gail Mandel
DESIGNER: BTDNYC

LIBRARY OF CONGRESS CATALOGING-IN-PUBLICATION DATA

Pisano, Dominick, 1943-
    Charles Lindbergh and the Spirit of St. Louis / By Dominick A. Pisano and F. Robert van der Linden;
    foreword by Reeve Lindbergh; new photography by Eric Long and Mark Avino.
        p. cm.
    Includes bibliographical references and index.
    ISBN 0-8109-0552-3 (hardcover)
    1. Lindbergh, Charles A. (Charles Augusutus), 1902-1974. 2. Spirit of St. Louis (Airplane)
    3. Transatlantic flights. 4. Aeronautics—Records. 5. Air pilots—United States—Biography.
    I. van der Linden, F. Robert. II. Title.
    TL540.L5 P57 2002
    629.13'092—dc21

                                                    2001006250

Copyright © 2002 Smithsonian Institution

Published in 2002 by Harry N. Abrams, Incorporated, New York.
All rights reserved. No part of the contents of this book may be reproduced
without the written permission of the publisher.

Printed and bound in Hong Kong

10 9 8 7 6 5 4 3 2 1

HARRY N. ABRAMS, INC.
100 FIFTH AVENUE
NEW YORK, N.Y. 10011
www.abramsbooks.com

ABRAMS IS A SUBSIDIARY OF

CONTENTS

FOREWORD

MY FATHER, Charles Lindbergh, and the *Spirit of St. Louis*, the little high-winged Ryan monoplane in which he flew from New York to Paris in 1927, are indivisible in the American imagination. It does not matter that my father piloted many other airplanes both before and after the famous 1927 flight. Nobody remembers any of them as well, not even the Lockheed Sirius seaplane with the unpronounceable Inuit name, *Tingmissartoq* (the one who flies like a big bird), in which he and my mother, Anne Morrow Lindbergh, made historic flights of exploration in the 1930s, charting air routes for the aviation industry all over the world.

The *Spirit of St. Louis* and its pilot were together for fewer than five hundred flying hours, over the course of barely a year. Only about thirty-three of those hours remain in our collective memory, but that memory is so tenacious that in his later years, during the time I knew him, my father would sometimes sigh as the month of May approached each year, and comment ruefully, "They just keep flying me to Paris."

It is still true. Even now, more than a quarter of a century after his death, celebrations continue to take place around the country on May 21, the day my father and the *Spirit of St. Louis* landed at Le Bourget field. Every year, the old black and white newsreels again flicker with the images of a young man and a silver airplane, fused together in one moment, forever.

The lingering idea that there was a special relationship between the man and the machine is a romantic one, perhaps a bit of hyperbole from a more romantic time, or a holdover from the myths of the American West, with lone cowboys on loyal horses riding into the sunset. My father played down this notion, insisting that *We*, the title of the book he wrote immediately after the flight, referred not to himself and the airplane but to the group of St. Louis businessmen who put up the money for the venture. Yet twenty-six years after he made the flight, while writing what he considered to be the more accurate and truly definitive account of that experience, his Pulitzer prize-winning book, *The Spirit of St. Louis*, my father described the airplane in these terms, "It's like a living creature, gliding along smoothly, happily, as though a successful flight means as much to it as to me, as though we shared our experiences together, each feeling beauty, life, and death as keenly, each dependent on the other's loyalty. We have made this flight across the ocean, not I or it." Readers will draw their own conclusions.

I did not know Charles Lindbergh in the ways that the world seems to know him best: as a pioneer pilot, as an American hero, as a controversial political figure before the Second World War, as a "lone" and solitary, enigmatic individual. I was born after all the famous history, and I knew him as a real person. He was my father, half of a strong parental presence in the large, busy family in which I grew up in the 1950s. I knew him then as a man of strong character and thoughtful opinion, shy and reserved in public but open and affectionate at home. I remember him now as a man perpetually in motion, exploring and thinking and talking and growing, throughout his life. I came to understand him, finally, as an American who represented his era and his nation in many ways, and who outgrew his own image many times, before he died in 1974. I believe that my father, above all, was a man who grew.

When I look for him now, however, I often go back to this flight and this airplane, and I find something essential in the story of the *Spirit of St. Louis*, marking the very beginning of my father's journey, one so much longer than the Atlantic crossing in the *Spirit*. The tale as Dominick A. Pisano and F. Robert van der Linden tell it here, with care and respect for both the man and the machine, speaks to me not just of my father and his airplane, but also of our country itself, of all we have accomplished in the past, all we have struggled with along the way, and all that lies ahead.

I am reminded of something else my father wrote, in his preface to *The Spirit of St. Louis*, and can think of no more fitting words with which to introduce this book: "We actually live, today, in our dreams of yesterday; and, living in those dreams, we dream again."

REEVE LINDBERGH
2001

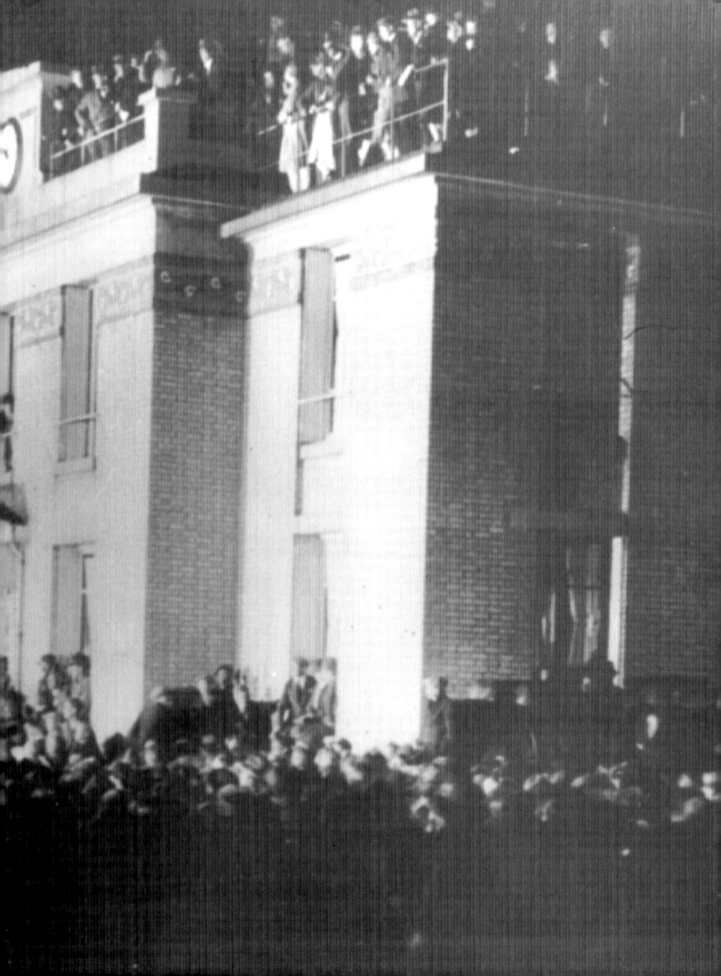

We

THIRTY-THREE HOURS SINCE TAKEOFF. It has been more than two days since he last slept, but Charles Lindbergh is no longer tired. Lindbergh, the son of a congressman, child of the Minnesota plains, barnstormer, and pioneer airmail pilot, is only thirty minutes away from the completion of his dream: to become the first person to fly nonstop, alone, across the Atlantic from New York to Paris.

His body and mind numbed by the incessant droning of the powerful engine, Lindbergh has nevertheless been alert since reaching the Irish coast five hours earlier. The rush of excitement knowing that he has conquered the ocean's hazards has defeated the overwhelming urge to sleep. It is two hours since he crossed over southwest England, and he is right on course. A while ago Lindbergh put away the Mercator charts with which he navigated a great circle route across the Atlantic and now, having crossed the English Channel at Cherbourg and making landfall later at Deauville, he is flying from a French railway map. The way to his final destination at Le Bourget airport is clear. For the first time since he left Roosevelt Field in Westbury, Long Island, just before eight o'clock in the morning of May 20, 1927, the twenty-five-year-old reaches into the stained brown bag next to him for one of the ham sandwiches he brought with him but, with his senses dulled by the hours aloft, he can barely taste it. It matters little; Lindbergh realizes that he has to focus on the job at hand. He briefly ponders the fate of French aviators Charles Nungesser and François Coli, who have not been heard from since they took off from Paris thirteen days before in their plane, *L' Oiseau Blanc.* Perhaps they have gone down in the vast Atlantic. Maybe they were able to land in a remote area of Canada and are awaiting rescue. He quietly wishes them the best and reflects on how easy it could have been for him to lose his fight with sleep and plunge into the ocean or succumb to a myriad other challenges that confront pilots in these early years of aviation.

Previous spread:
A huge crowd of more than 150,000 onlookers gather at Le Bourget airport minutes before Lindbergh's arrival. Thanks to the recently introduced wirephoto, of which this is an example, Americans were able to see the scene of the landing immediately.

The last half hour, though flown as dusk fades into night over unfamiliar territory, is not difficult. As is just beginning to happen in the United States, major airlanes in Europe are well lit by beacons, especially between London and Paris. With no windscreen and limited forward vision, Lindbergh climbs to four thousand feet to avoid dangerous obstructions, flying over the heads of farmers and their families who look up from their Normandy homes in the patchwork of fields and hedgerows that will ensnare an Allied army seventeen years hence. From this altitude the lights of each passed village are visible on this clear evening. With the eerie green glow returning to the luminescent dials in his cockpit, Lindbergh should return to instrument flying, but with the gleaming City of Lights just up ahead and the river Seine below, it seems unnecessary. Only a sudden engine failure can keep him from reaching his destination. Once again Lindbergh checks the magneto switches and once again everything is fine—his Wright Whirlwind is running as well now as when he left New York. The engine did quit once, but that was four hours ago over St. George's Channel, between Wales and southern Ireland, when Lindbergh forgot to switch fuel tanks and let his nose tank run dry. He had plenty of fuel left in the other three tanks, however, and when he remembered to open a valve to the center wing tank in his high-wing monoplane, the trusty engine sputtered back to life.

With Paris in sight, Lindbergh is almost sorry that he will be landing. Since September he has been planning for this moment, and now that it has arrived he does not wish for the journey to end. But end it must. For, though he has enough gasoline to fly another thousand miles and though his valiant Ryan NY-P aircraft will do his bidding, his goal lies just ahead. Lindbergh navigates his silver fabric–covered monoplane down the famous Champs-Elysées to the Eiffel Tower. Le Bourget is nearby, but Lindbergh does not know exactly where. No one he asked in the U.S. knew its precise location, only that it lay northeast of the city.

The minutes pass and there are no beacons leading him to a major airfield. Realizing that he may be above the beacon, Lindbergh turns his attention to locating a large piece of dark land when he passes over a field illuminated with spotlights and thousands of smaller lights from what must be nearby factories. Unsure, he flies on for a few minutes until he sees nothing else, and turns back. Indeed, it is Le Bourget. What he thought were factory lights are in fact the lights of thousands of automobiles trapped in traffic struggling to meet him. He spirals down and sees that the spotlights are illuminating a huge airfield. Soon he finds the windsock and, in a gentle ten-mile-per-hour wind, begins his descent, diving to lose altitude until he is lined up in his approach over the floodlights and into the wind.

After circling the field one last time, Lindbergh throttles back. His reflexes are now quite dull from fatigue, and he finds himself struggling to control his aircraft. Sideslipping the Ryan to lose speed and altitude, Lindbergh is concerned that he is still coming in too fast and will overshoot his landing. At eighty miles per hour he is fast, and now that the *Spirit* is lightly loaded from burning off 365 of the 450 gallons of fuel with which it started the flight, the craft still wishes to fly. Pressing on, he makes one last trim adjustment to his horizontal stabilizer, pulls the nose up a little, flares his aircraft as carefully as he can, and, after several gentle bounces, settles

Wirephoto. The French military and police officials cordon off the *Spirit of St. Louis* to prevent further damage to the plane by the overly-enthusiastic crowd.

safely to earth and into history. His journey has covered 3,610 miles in thirty-three hours and thirty minutes.

France is overwhelmed and so is Lindbergh. Expecting no one to greet him and concerned about arriving without a visa, Lindbergh has letters of introduction. They are unnecessary. He is also concerned that anti-American resentment will have been aroused by the disappearance of Nungesser and Coli. He need not worry. He is immediately embraced by exuberant Frenchmen who surround the *Spirit of St. Louis* and try to carry Lindbergh away on their shoulders. In the crush his helmet disappears, last

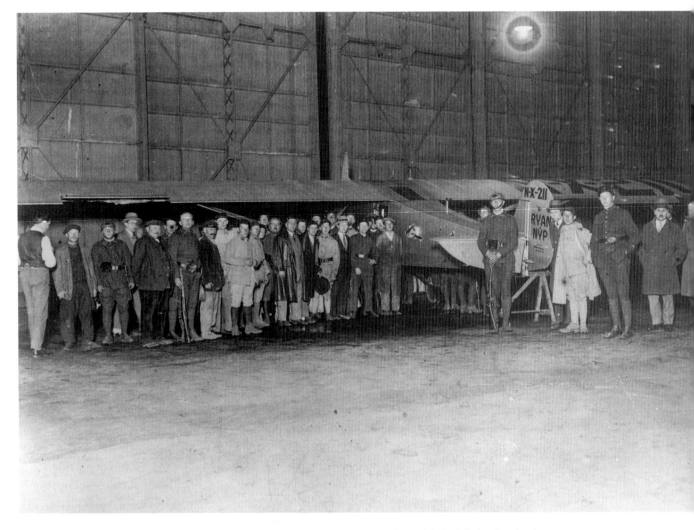

Wirephoto. With fabric torn from its fuselage and control surfaces by souvenir hunters, the *Spirit of St. Louis* finds refuge in a hangar at Le Bourget airport.

seen on the head of a reporter who is later mistaken for the American pilot. Lindbergh is rescued by two of France's most distinguished aviators, Major Michel Detroyat and Gustave Delage. They see to it that the pilot is immediately cared for and that the *Spirit* is secured after only minor damage from the grasping hands of souvenir hunters. His escorts whisk Lindbergh first to U.S. Ambassador Myron T. Herrick and later through the backroads of Paris to the safety and serenity of the American embassy, where, at half past four on the morning of May 21, 1927, Lindbergh finally goes to sleep. He has been awake for sixty-three hours straight.

FROM THAT MOMENT ON, Charles Lindbergh became a public figure. His quiet strength and dignity were in direct opposition to the crass "ballyhoo" era of the so-called Roaring Twenties. This tall, slender American possessed the best human qualities of courage, determination, and reserve. Overnight, Lindbergh became the most popular and most recognized person on the planet. His great flight across the ocean helped pave the way for the expansion of commercial aviation around the globe and opened new horizons for the world. His fame would come at a great personal cost to him and his family, yet he remained stoic in the face of adversity, even when his own personal views differed greatly from those of the majority of his fellow Americans.

Much is known about Charles Lindbergh; countless books and articles have chronicled his life from every imaginable perspective. Seventy-five years after his flight, the public remains fascinated with this complex person. But what of his aircraft? And what of his skills as a pilot? All of Lindbergh's strength and determination would have come to naught if his *Spirit of St. Louis* had failed, or his flight training had proven inadequate. Lindbergh and his aircraft were one. Together they achieved what no one had done before, and for this Lindbergh forever referred to his aircraft and himself as "We."

Pictured in Paris from left to right are Lindbergh, President of France Gaston Doumergue, and United States Ambassador to France Myron T. Herrick.

The Man

"Me and My Best Chum"

Charles A. Lindbergh is pictured with Dr. Charles H. Land, his maternal grandfather. A well-known dentist, Dr. Land taught the young Charles that "Science is the key to all mystery."

CHARLES A. LINDBERGH was born in Detroit on February 4, 1902, to Charles Augustus (C. A.) Lindbergh, Sr. and Evangeline Lodge Land. Lindbergh's paternal grandfather, Ola Manson (on coming to America he changed his name to August Lindbergh), immigrated to the United States from Sweden in 1860 and helped to establish Melrose, a small community in south central Minnesota. August Lindbergh was known for his independence, honesty, and stoicism, traits that he passed on to Lindbergh's father and to Lindbergh himself.

Lindbergh's father was a lawyer with a reputation for helping needy farmers with loans of money to stave off foreclosure. He became involved in local politics and in 1906 was elected to the U.S. House of Representatives from Minnesota's Sixth District, serving until 1916. As Lindbergh biographer Kenneth S. Davis describes him, C. A. was "a tall, lean, fair-complexioned man, loosely but powerfully built, with a long lean face, high cheekbones, a stubbornly determined jaw, and a full mouth that was rarely broadened into a smile. His eyes were

Opposite: Lindbergh (left) dislocated his shoulder after making an emergency parachute jump from an airplane near Lambert Field in St. Louis in 1925. The man at the right is unidentified. Lindbergh began his flying career as a wing walker and parachute jumper. He went on to become a barnstorming pilot traveling from town to town giving flying demonstrations, performing stunts, and taking passengers into the air for a fee.

of a clear blue. Through them he looked out directly upon the world but into them few men could ever look very far, for it was as if a shutter dropped down behind them when personal matters arose. His was a Puritan's countenance: to those who knew him only casually (he permitted few to know him better) his facial expression often seemed frozen in a Nordic hostility to all joy, all beauty, all the warm spontaneities of Southern natures."[1]

As a youth Lindbergh spent much of his time in Little Falls, Minnesota, and in Washington, D.C., where he visited his father once a year. His growing-up years were characterized by an interest in the outdoors and things mechanical and scientific. C. A. had taught the young Charles how to handle himself in the Minnesota wilderness, and, above all, to be self-sufficient. When he was eleven years old, Lindbergh learned to drive the family car, and by the age of fourteen was chauffeuring his father on campaign tours in Minnesota. By the age of sixteen he had assumed complete responsibility for operating the family farm, using his mechanical ability to keep things in repair. He also developed an interest in aviation, having been excited by an air show that he had seen at Fort Myer, Virginia, and by an itinerant barnstormer who had passed through Little Falls.

In the fall of 1920, Lindbergh entered the University of Wisconsin. Although he had dreamed of entering the Massachusetts Institute of Technology to study aeronautical engineering (MIT had one of the earliest programs in that field), his high-school grades were only fair, and he had to settle for studying mechanical engineering on a probationary basis. During his time at the University of Wisconsin, Lindbergh was undistinguished in his schoolwork. He preferred to ride his Excelsior motorcycle, which he had acquired while in high school, recklessly touring the country roads in the areas surrounding Madison. He and two companions, Delos Dudley and Richard Plummer, also built an iceboat and sailed it on a nearby lake. He became the marksman of the Reserve Officer Training Corps rifle team, scoring fifty bull's-eyes in a row in competition matches. He had no interest in girls or campus social life (he did not have a single date the entire time he was in college), lived in relative isolation, and had no friends, except for Dudley and Plummer, who shared his passion for machinery. After a year and a half at Wisconsin, Lindbergh dropped out of school and decided to seek his fortune as a pilot.

Lindbergh had solicited literature from various flying schools and was especially impressed by the brochures of the Nebraska Aircraft Corporation in Lincoln. This company manufactured the Lincoln Standard biplane and offered flight instruction. In April 1922, Lindbergh traveled to Lincoln to enroll in flight training, for which he paid a sum of five hundred dollars. He soon realized that the training offered by the company was rather sketchy, if not downright fraudulent, and that he was the sole student. His instructor, Ira Biffle, was a disinterested pilot, and Lindbergh flew only eight hours over a period of six weeks and was not allowed to solo. Nevertheless, it was here that he began to learn to fly and become familiar with the construction of aircraft and the protocols of the flying field.

In Lincoln, Lindbergh had met Erold Bahl, a barnstormer who was considered the best pilot in Lincoln. He convinced Bahl that he should be allowed to accompany the pilot on his next barnstorming tour (barnstorming was a theatrical term—referring to touring dramatic troupes that performed in barns—that was applied to itinerant pilots who flew from town to town giving flying demonstrations, performing stunts, and taking passengers into the air for a fee), even suggesting that he would do it without pay. Bahl agreed, and soon Lindbergh was making himself useful by working on Bahl's airplane and surveying the crowds for potential passengers. Bahl was duly impressed and began to pay Lindbergh for his services. It was during his time with Bahl, and later with Charles W. Hardin, that Lindbergh began the risky business of wing-walking and parachute jumping. About these dangerous activities Lindbergh later wrote, "there were lots of tricks in exhibition work—closely guarded secrets of professional circus flyers. Ownership of a parachute made me an apprentice in the craft, and gave me the right to be taught its skills. I'd made friends with a young mechanic named Pete . . . . It was from him I learned that a wing walker didn't really hang by his teeth from a leather strap attached to the landing gear's spreader bar. He simply held the strap in his mouth while his weight was safely supported by a steel cable hooked to a strong harness underneath his coat. The cable was too thin for eyes on the ground to see, and the effect on the crowd was as good as though none were there. Certainly that didn't involve much danger, yet men who hung 'by their teeth' from airplanes were called daredevils."[2]

Commenting on Lindbergh's attitude toward risk-taking, Kenneth Davis says that fliers of the period often appeared to be "seemingly indifferent to the dangers to which they exposed themselves, and often appeared equally so to the dangers they imposed on others. Many of them manifested a quality of cold insensitivity in their human relations, as if they had become identified in essential ways with the machines they flew and so had lost much of their capacity for human feeling." Davis goes on to cite two published accounts by Lindbergh of his early flying experiences

Ormer Leslie Locklear, a barnstormer of the 1920s, performs one of the daredevil stunts in the barnstorming repertoire.

in which he seems to express the same sense of distance from other people, particularly nonfliers. Nevertheless, the feats Lindbergh performed were not only difficult physically but also emotionally because he had to overcome the fear generated by recurring nightmares as a child of falling from great heights.[3]

In July through October of 1922, Lindbergh continued his barnstorming activities with two other men, H. J. "Cupid" Lynch, a pilot, and "Banty" Rogers, a Kansas wheat farmer still learning to fly, who owned the Lincoln Standard they flew on tour. The team proceeded through western Kansas, eastern Colorado, Wyoming, and Montana. Lindbergh described his experiences in these words: "'DAREDEVIL LINDBERGH'—that's how I was billed, in huge black letters on the colored posters we threw out above towns and villages. People came for miles to watch me climb back and forth over wings, and finally leap off into space. Ranchers, cowboys, storekeepers in town, followed with their eyes as I walked by. Had I been 'Liver-Eating Johnson' I could hardly have been accorded more prestige. Shooting and gunplay those people understood; but a man who'd willingly jump off an airplane's wing had a disdain for death that was beyond them."[4]

In April 1923, Lindbergh journeyed to Souther Field near Americus, Georgia, to purchase his first airplane. Although he had been involved a great deal in barnstorming the previous year, he had yet to solo, and he was anxious to have his own airplane. He bought a World War I surplus Curtiss JN-4 "Jenny" with a Curtiss OX-5 engine, the preferred and affordable choice of many barnstorming pilots in the United States. The perils of flying his own aircraft soon became manifest to Lindbergh. On his first flight, intending to make only a few practice hops, Lindbergh misjudged the airplane's handling characteristics and had a near-crash on landing. A pilot named Henderson offered to take the embarrassed Lindbergh up in the Jenny for practice takeoffs and landings. After a few rough liftoffs and touchdowns, Henderson suggested that Lindbergh take the airplane up himself, which he did. At dusk in the vicinity of the Chatahoochee River, he flew over Americus. After a brief but satisfying flight, Lindbergh successfully landed the airplane, having made his first solo flight.

During this time, Lindbergh had other near-misses. After leaving Souther Field, Lindbergh made his way south toward Meridian, Mississippi, where he got lost and had to land in a pasture. He taxied too fast across a grass-covered ditch, his airplane nosed over, and he damaged his propeller. Shortly afterward, he flew through Arkansas into Texas, and from there into Oklahoma and Kansas. As he approached the town of Alma, about twenty-five miles west of Topeka, he landed in a field where tall grass concealed limestone ridges and loose rocks, and ground-looped the airplane, damaging its left wing. Later, as he was flying from Nebraska to Minnesota, he approached Shakopee, southwest of Minneapolis, in a rainstorm, where he had intended to land but could not. He continued eastward toward Savage, where he had engine trouble and was forced to land in a swamp. The wheels of the aircraft sank deeply into the mud; it nosed over, leaving Lindbergh hanging upside down by his safety belt, and the propeller and spreader bar damaged. Finally, on a campaign tour in which he had intended to fly his father from place to place in Minnesota during C. A.'s unsuccessful race for U.S. Senator, Lindbergh, with his father in the front seat, crashed on takeoff from Litchfield. Accounts vary about the cause: some claim the aircraft hit tall grass and nosed over; some say it took a nosedive after taking off. An eyewitness who was a friend of C. A.'s was quoted as saying that the plane "had a fall fifty feet from the ground" and recollected that C. A. "had many blows in [sic] his head . . . his glasses was broken and we washed blood from his face."[5]

After attending the International Air Races at Lambert Field in St. Louis in the fall of 1923, where he saw Lt. Alford Williams, U.S.N., set an international speed record of 243.67 MPH, Lindbergh met and began teaching Leon Klink, a young automobile dealer, to fly Klink's Canuck, the Canadian version of the Jenny. Lindbergh and Klink set off from Lambert Field on a barnstorming odyssey that would take them into Missouri, Kentucky, Tennessee, Mississippi, Alabama, Florida, Louisiana, and Texas, and, again, Lindbergh put his life in danger. Flying alone near Pensacola, Florida, he developed engine trouble and crash landed, smashing the propeller and tearing the landing gear from the airplane.

Next, while flying in southwestern Texas, Lindbergh and Klink, short of fuel, were forced to land in a small pasture that would not allow them to take off again carrying both men. Alone, Lindbergh flew the plane to the nearby town square of Camp Wood. In attempting to take off from one of the town's streets, Lindbergh had to maneuver the aircraft's forty-four-foot wingspan between telephone poles placed forty-six feet apart. The result was predictable. The aircraft caught a rough spot in the street and was spun around, the wing tip catching a pole and driving nose-first into the wall of a hardware store.

Finally, a few days later, near the town of Maxon, Texas, Lindbergh and Klink had to hack their way through brush and cactus to clear a path for the aircraft to take off. Because of thin air, the aircraft could not clear the vegetation, and its lower wing was damaged so severely that Lindbergh was forced to make an emergency landing. Klink had to travel to El Paso to get the necessary material to repair the aircraft. The two had been on the ground for more than a week, and Lindbergh needed to get to Brooks Field, Texas, by March 15 to enlist as an aviation cadet and enter U.S. Army flight training. In January 1924, realizing that barnstorming was not a profitable way of making a living, he had taken the entrance examinations at Chanute Field, Illinois.

Although military flight training was demanding, for the first time in his life Lindbergh felt that he had a real purpose, and applied himself rigorously. It was here that he learned maintenance, radio, photography, meteorology, and, of greatest importance for his future career, navigation, including the intricacies of reading a variety of maps and learning to steer by compass.

As Kenneth Davis characterizes it, "his grade record indicates the seriousness with which, for the first time in his life, he studied school assignments, spending hours over his books on weekends and studying, often until late night. Through ground school he was driven by three motives of apparently equal strength: desire to learn, ambition to succeed, fear of failure. Only the first two operated, however, when he climbed into a plane." This last statement was undoubtedly true because with every flight Lindbergh was courting danger. During the course of his flight training he was involved in a stunting incident with a deHavilland aircraft in which both pilots were flying too low. Lindbergh was afraid that he might be "washed out" of flight school, but no action was taken against him. Then, a few days before his graduation from flight school, Lindbergh, flying an SE-5, collided with a pilot named C. D. McAllister in another SE-5, forcing both of them to parachute out of their aircraft. Lindbergh and McAllister thus became the twelfth and thirteenth members (respectively) of the exclusive so-called "Caterpillar Club"—pilots who had parachuted out of airplanes.[6]

In March 1925, after Lindbergh finished his military pilot training, he was commissioned a second lieutenant in the U.S. Army Air Service Reserve. He had graduated at the top of his class, one of only eighteen men who remained from the original group of one hundred four. Kenneth Davis says that Lindbergh had begun to experience changes in his life. "Along with a vast increase in his flying knowledge and skill, the Army has given him a sense of professional responsibility. There is even (and this will swiftly grow) a dedication to aviation as a Cause. In consequence of this, the wild recklessness which marked so many of his earlier flying experiences, and which almost certainly would have killed him within a few years had it not been checked, will from now on be less evident in his actions. He will still run grave risks; he will still seek the thrills of danger. But from now on the risks will be more carefully calculated and his thrill-seeking propensities will be curbed by sober judgment."[7]

After flight training Lindbergh went to St. Louis, where he had been hired by Frank and William Robertson of the Robertson Aircraft Corporation, to be the company's chief pilot. Since the federal contracts to carry the mail would not be awarded until later that year, Lindbergh decided not to wait around, and instead went back to barnstorming, flying through Illinois, Missouri, and Iowa in the spring of 1925. In May of that year, his courage was tested once more when, some three hundred feet from the ground, he was forced to parachute out of an OXX-6

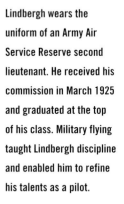

Lindbergh wears the uniform of an Army Air Service Reserve second lieutenant. He received his commission in March 1925 and graduated at the top of his class. Military flying taught Lindbergh discipline and enabled him to refine his talents as a pilot.

Plywood Special, a four-passenger aircraft designed by an aeronautical engineer named Ben Belle. This jump nearly cost him his life because the aircraft's propeller came within feet of hitting him as the plane made its way to earth. He escaped with minor injuries and a dislocated shoulder, becoming a two-time member of the Caterpillar Club.

After spending some time on active duty at Richards Field, Missouri, in July 1925, Lindbergh went to Denver to join the Mil-Hi Airways and Flying Circus so that he could, as he put it, have "a chance to explore the air currents around canyons, slopes, and ridges. I could study the effect of turbulence, about which aviators knew so little and speculated so much." Lindbergh also barnstormed eastern Colorado, and near Lamar he claimed to have cured a man who was hard of hearing by taking him up beyond seven thousand feet, and then diving to earth in multiple spins: "he was sure sick and couldn't hear as well as before but the next day his hearing was noticeably improved. . . ." Despite this lighthearted episode, Lindbergh was involved in another close call when on a flight near Fowler, Colorado, he was caught in a severe windstorm and nearly ran out of fuel attempting to land. Although he landed the aircraft perfectly, he characterized the experience to J. Wray Vaughn, owner of Mil-Hi: "You can put that down in the book . . . I've never been scared like that before."[8]

In late 1925, Robertson Aircraft Corporation received its airmail contract (CAM-2), and Lindbergh went to work for the company in earnest, flying the route between St. Louis and Chicago. Lindbergh's job as chief pilot was to plan the route and recruit other pilots to fly the company's small fleet of converted deHavilland DH-4Bs. His first two hires were his army buddies Philip Love and Thomas Nelson.

Working diligently through the autumn and winter of 1925 and into the spring of 1926, Lindbergh's preparations paid off. On April 15, 1926, Lindbergh piloted the inaugural flight of the Robertson Aircraft Corporation. Soon he was managing a smoothly functioning organization despite the hazards of bad weather, night flying, and mechanical breakdowns. The temperamental surplus Liberty engines failed with annoying frequency, and the lack of navigational aids hampered operations. Nevertheless, Robertson—a predecessor of today's American Airlines—still managed to deliver 99 percent of the airmail on time. During this period Lindbergh learned to trust his rudimentary instruments; no mean feat for a pilot trained to fly on instinct alone. Flying in fog or cloud cost many a disoriented pilot his life. An altimeter and turn-and-bank indicator often disagreed with what the pilot felt, but were invariably correct. This hard lesson would later save Lindbergh's life.

In his book *The Spirit of St. Louis*, Lindbergh recalled his experiences at Robertson. "Three of us carry on this service: Philip Love, Thomas Nelson, and I. We've established the best record of all the routes converging at Chicago, with over ninety-nine percent of our scheduled flights completed. Ploughing through storms, wedging our way beneath low clouds, paying almost no attention to weather forecasts, we've more than once landed our rebuilt army warplanes on Chicago's Maywood field when other lines canceled out, when older and perhaps wiser pilots ordered their cargo put on a train. During the long days of summer we seldom missed a flight. But now winter is creeping up on us. Nights are lengthening; skies are thickening with haze and storm. We're already landing by floodlight at Chicago. In a few more weeks it will be dark when we glide down onto that narrow strip of cow pasture called the Peoria stop along the route airmail field. Before the winter is past, even the meadow at Springfield will need lights." The job was inherently dangerous. On September 16, 1926, and again on November 3, 1926, Lindbergh was forced to bail out of his aircraft, making him the first four-time member of the Caterpillar Club.[9]

In September 1926, on an airmail flight from Peoria to Chicago, Lindbergh began to think seriously about the possibility of flying across the Atlantic. For some

Lindbergh poses in front of his Douglas M-4 mail plane. At the time he was chief pilot for the Robertson Aircraft Corporation, an airmail contract firm in St. Louis. It was during an airmail flight that Lindbergh became convinced that he could fly across the Atlantic.

months he had been aware of the competition for the Orteig Prize, the $25,000 award to the first aviator to fly nonstop from New York to Paris or Paris to New York in a heavier-than-air craft.

IN 1902, THE YEAR OF LINDBERGH'S BIRTH, a French-born former maitre d' named Raymond Orteig had purchased the Brevoort Hotel on Fifth Avenue between East 8th and 9th Streets in New York, renovated it, and made it into a haven for Greenwich Village artists and writers. In the same year, he also purchased the nearby Lafayette Hotel at University Place and East 9th Street, which became a watering hole for international celebrities drawn by Orteig's carefully selected menus and wine lists. During World War I, he became enthralled by the adventuresome "Knights of the Air." Orteig was fascinated by the chivalry of the pilots, especially that displayed by the Lafayette Escadrille, a group of American volunteers who flew for France, who were likened to Galahad, Roland, and Lancelot in the popular imagination.

Beyond this, Orteig, like Jacques Schneider, who had offered the Schneider Cup in the hope of encouraging overwater flying in 1913, believed that the future of aviation lay in the peaceful pursuit of transoceanic flying. So, in 1919, through the Aero Club of America, Orteig decided to offer a prize of $25,000 "to the first aviator who shall cross the Atlantic in a land or water aircraft (heavier-than-air) from Paris or the shores of France to New York, or from New York to Paris or the shores of France, without stop," with the stipulation that the flight be made within five years. In April 1913, Alfred Harmsworth (later Lord Northcliffe), owner of the London *Daily Mail, Times,* and *Daily Mirror* newspapers had offered a £10,000 prize for the first person to cross the Atlantic in an airplane, from any point in Great Britain or Ireland to any point in Newfoundland, Canada, or the United States.[10]

While no transatlantic flights were made that conformed to the New York–Paris/Paris–New York requirement laid down by Orteig, it is estimated that 117 people traveled by air across the Atlantic, most as passengers, before Lindbergh successfully made his solo crossing in May 1927. The first crossing, on June 14, 1919, flown by two British aviators, Captain John Alcock and Lt. Arthur Whitten Brown in a Vickers Vimy, from Trespassy Bay, St. John's, Newfoundland, to Clifden, Ireland, was a difficult 1,936-mile affair that took fifteen hours, fifty-seven minutes, nonstop. In completing their flight, Alcock and Brown won the *Daily Mail* prize. About a month earlier, in May 1919, U.S. Navy Curtiss NC flying boats, led by Lt. Cdr. Albert C. Read, made the crossing from St. John's, Newfoundland, to the Azores, to Lisbon,

to Plymouth, England, in approximately three weeks. Only one of the aircraft, the NC-4, completed the flight. In July 1919, the British airship R-34 completed the first successful airship crossing of the Atlantic. In 1924, in their around-the-world flight, three Army Air Service Douglas World Cruisers crossed the Atlantic, going from Nova Scotia to Brough, England, by way of Greenland and Iceland.

Meanwhile, in the five years since Orteig had offered it, nobody had been able to do what was required to win the prize, primarily because the technological limitations of aircraft would not allow it, so Orteig renewed it for an additional five years. The most significant technological breakthrough that would ensure the eventual conquest of the Atlantic Ocean by air came in the early 1920s with the development of a reliable, lightweight, air-cooled power plant. With the advent of the aircraft carrier, the U.S. Navy had to find an engine that could produce sufficient power without the serious drawbacks of existing water-cooled motors. Concerned that current water-cooled engines were too heavy and susceptible to breakdown and battle damage because of their vulnerable radiators and hoses, the Navy became increasingly interested in the J series of air-cooled engines produced by the tiny Lawrance Aero-Engine Corporation of New York City.

Seeking a large company with the resources to produce and develop this engine, the Navy pressured the Wright Aeronautical Corporation in Paterson, New Jersey, into purchasing the Lawrance company in 1923. By 1924, the Wright J-3

Eight years before Lindbergh's solo flight, Captain John Alcock and Lieutenant Arthur Whitten Brown crossed the Atlantic in a Vickers Vimy. Their 1,936-mile journey took slightly less than sixteen hours.

One of Lindbergh's competitors for the Orteig Prize was World War I French ace René Fonck. Here, Fonck (right) and Igor Sikorsky wave from the cockpit of the Sikorsky S-35 transatlantic aircraft.

and J-4 Whirlwind engines were in production and providing reliable service not only to the Navy but to civilians as well. The Wright J-5 engine, which was the first to employ Englishman Samuel D. Heron's revolutionary sodium-cooled valves, virtually eliminated the chronic problem of burned exhaust valves. The engine's self-lubricating rocker arms removed the constant need to grease these crucial parts. These two features made the Wright J-5 the world's first truly reliable, modern aircraft engine and one that could last hundreds, if not thousands of hours between overhauls and failures. It could fly from New York to Paris.

No one, however, had successfully crossed the Atlantic nonstop in an airplane since Alcock and Brown in 1919, and the distance between New York and Paris was sixteen hundred miles farther than they had flown. By September 1926, it appeared that the French ace René Fonck and a crew of three were ready to compete for the prize. They took off in a three-engine Sikorsky S-35 biplane, but the aircraft, loaded down with fuel and baggage and encumbered with supplementary landing gear, crashed on takeoff when the second gear failed. Fonck's mechanic and wireless operator were killed, but he and his copilot, Lawrence Curtin, managed to escape. By 1927, Lindbergh had some strong competitors, including Commander Richard

Byrd, U.S.N.; Noel Davis and Stanton Wooster, naval aviators with much experience; Clarence Chamberlin, another seasoned pilot, and Charles Levine, his financial backer and owner of the aircraft; and French ace Charles Nungesser and François Coli. Lindbergh's competitors had been driven by various factors, including the renewal of the Orteig Prize and improvements in engine technology. The most important development at the time, however, was a pilot's ability to receive a weather forecast for the North Atlantic coupled with the fact that May was the earliest one could expect favorable flying conditions over the route.

In Lindbergh's mind the only possibility of success lay in a solo flight across the Atlantic: "I'll fly alone. That will cut out the need for any selection of crew, or quarreling. If there's upholstery in the cabin, I'll tear it out for the flight. I'll take only the food I need to eat, and a few concentrated rations. I'll carry a rubber boat for emergency, and a little extra water." Lindbergh had thought about Fonck's attempt in the Sikorsky S-35. The aircraft was fitted with three new powerful Wright Whirlwind engines. While known for their reliability, with a time between overhaul of 250 hours, Lindbergh did not see that three provided any more margin of safety than one. In his thinking, this only tripled the chances of an engine failure, no matter how good the power plant.[11]

What Lindbergh found most troubling, however, was the fact that Fonck had been carrying so much useless weight. Why carry four men when at most two were necessary? Certainly the bed and red leather appointments were not needed, nor were the two shortwave and longwave radios, let alone the gifts and facilities to cook hot meals, which the press reported he was carrying.

Lindbergh concluded that the Atlantic Ocean could be conquered with a much smaller, modern, single-engine aircraft, with a minimum of equipment and only one pilot. The new Wright-Bellanca, an already existing single-engine airplane designed and built by Giuseppe Bellanca, a noted aircraft designer and manufacturer, and

Other competitors for the Orteig Prize included the World War I French ace Charles Nungesser (right) and his copilot François Coli, a highly decorated veteran pilot of World War I. On May 8, 1927, the two took off from Le Bourget airport in Paris in their aircraft, *L'Oiseau Blanc,* but they disappeared over the Atlantic and were never found.

powered by a Wright Whirlwind radial engine, fitted the bill perfectly. Only now Lindbergh had to find a way to persuade the company to sell him their airplane. Having convinced himself of the possibility of the flight and, with almost two thousand hours already spent in the air, confident in his flying abilities, he now had to convince others to support him, for such an undertaking would require considerable cash. With two thousand dollars he had saved for emergencies, Lindbergh drafted a plan outlining the details of the proposed flight and what assistance he would need.

Lindbergh initially thought that the Wright-Bellanca, pictured here, was the ideal single-engine plane for his transatlantic flight. The pilot, however, eventually settled upon flying a craft constructed by Ryan Airlines.

Lindbergh arranged to see Earl Thompson, an insurance executive whom he had taught to fly, about financial backing. When he discussed the idea of purchasing the Wright-Bellanca with Thompson, Thompson listened intently, but questioned the fact that the aircraft would be a landplane, and suggested a flying boat or trimotor aircraft. Lindbergh explained the disadvantages of such craft, and by the end of the conversation, Thompson had become interested in the idea.

Lindbergh also toyed with the idea of having the Fokker company build the airplane, but when he spoke with a company representative about it the man suggested a price of $90,000 to $100,000 for a multi-engine aircraft. When Lindbergh persisted in his idea of a single-engine aircraft, he was turned down. This however did not deter Lindbergh, and he made an appointment to see Major Albert Bond Lambert, who had commanded a school for balloon pilots during World War I and was the owner of Lambert Field in St. Louis. Lambert promised Lindbergh one thousand dollars for the flight. He next went to his boss, Major Bill Robertson, to make arrangements to have someone fly his mail route while he was making the transatlantic flight. Although Robertson could not pledge financial support, he approved of the idea and suggested that the *St. Louis Post-Dispatch* might finance the flight.

An editor at the *Post-Dispatch* told Lindbergh that the paper would never finance such a dangerous flight, but this only strengthened Lindbergh's resolve. Lindbergh next visited the Wright Aeronautical Corporation, where he inquired about the possibility of acquiring the Whirlwind-powered Wright-Bellanca for the flight. He was told that the Bellanca had been built merely to demonstrate the capabilities of the Wright engine and was not available. The Wright company representative suggested that Lindbergh speak with the aircraft's designer, Giuseppe Bellanca, which he did the following evening at the Waldorf-Astoria Hotel in New York. While Bellanca made no commitment, Lindbergh left New York confident that Bellanca would support him.

He next visited Harry H. Knight of Knight, Dysart & Gamble, a brokerage firm in St. Louis. Knight asked Harold Bixby, a vice president of the State National Bank in St. Louis and president of the St. Louis Chamber of Commerce to consider joining him in financing the young pilot's attempt. In a matter of weeks, Knight and Bixby made the decision to back Lindbergh. While Lindbergh continued to look for a suitable craft, they came up with the $15,000 needed to finance the flight. It was Bixby who suggested to Lindbergh that he name his so-far-nonexistent aircraft the *Spirit of St. Louis.*

Not having heard from Bellanca, Lindbergh decided to inquire of the Travel Air Company in Wichita, Kansas, about an aircraft built to his specifications. Travel Air refused, so finally in February 1927 he contacted a tiny company in San Diego, Ryan Airlines, which had built mail planes for West Coast routes: "Can you construct Whirlwind engine plane capable flying nonstop between New York and Paris? STOP. If so please state cost and delivery date." Ryan replied that they could build an aircraft that met Lindbergh's needs, which would be similar to their model M, but with larger wings. Meanwhile, however, Giuseppe Bellanca wired encouragingly that he would be willing to make Lindbergh an "attractive proposition" concerning a New York–Paris aircraft. Lindbergh went at once to visit Clarence Chamberlin, pilot of Columbia Aircraft, Bellanca's affiliate and representative, with the money, to be told that the company would only close the deal if it had the right to select the crew that would fly the aircraft. The frustrated aviator departed, angry that he had wasted his time and money in attempting to obtain the Bellanca. At Bixby's urging, Lindbergh went to San Diego.[12]

The Plane

FOUNDED BY T. CLAUDE RYAN in September 1922, the Ryan Flying School first consisted of a single Curtiss JN-4 purchased from the army base commander Henry H. "Hap" Arnold at Rockwell Field in San Diego. Flying passengers, providing flight instruction, and selling aircraft barely paid the bills, but Ryan was able to expand his enterprise, albeit slowly. In 1923 he moved his operation from San Diego Bay to a larger and safer location next to the Marine Corps Recruiting Depot known as "Dutch Flats." There the young entrepreneur built a proper hangar and office in which his fledgling company could expand. Soon he hired his first mechanics, Hawley Bowlus and John van der Linde, the latter an emigrant from the Dutch East Indies.

Later that year, Ryan purchased six surplus Standard J-1 trainers. Bowlus and Ryan quickly reengined and widened the J-1s into enclosed-cabin airliners for use on a variety of tasks from sightseeing to charter trips and aerial advertising. The modified trainers actually exceeded all expectations and provided reliable and profitable service.

At this time, one of Ryan's students, B. F. (Benjamin Franklin) Mahoney, suggested a business partnership in order to create an airline between San Diego and Los Angeles. With Mahoney's financial support and Ryan's aircraft infrastructure, Ryan Airlines was formed in 1924. With Mahoney in Los Angeles and Ryan in San Diego, the new airline began service on March 1, 1925. In fact, the Los Angeles–San Diego carrier was the first U.S. airline to operate regularly scheduled year-round service. Initially quite successful, Ryan bought the much larger Davis-Douglas Cloudster (Donald Douglas's first aircraft) and modified it for passenger service. As the novelty of air travel wore off, however, costs mounted and Ryan and Mahoney turned their attention to manufacturing.

They saw an opportunity to market an aircraft smaller than the DH-4s, Curtiss Carrier Pigeons, and Douglas M-2s used on the heavily traveled primary routes and

The *Spirit of St. Louis* hangs on display in the Milestones of Flight gallery of the National Air and Space Museum.

more suited to the thinner secondary lines. Ryan quickly sketched preliminary plans for a diminutive parasol monoplane with a cockpit in front for two passengers or mail and the pilot's cockpit behind.

By early 1926 the Ryan M-1 took shape. Its fuselage was built of welded steel tubing and employed a highly effective Warren truss that made bracing wires unnecessary. The one-piece wing was made of wood and featured a Clark Y airfoil. Two steel struts covered with streamlined balsa-wood fairing braced each wing. The tail featured an adjustable horizontal stabilizer. The entire aircraft was covered in silver-doped cotton fabric. Power was provided by a single 150-horsepower Hispano-Suiza water-cooled V-8, although, wisely, the engine mounts were designed in such a manner as to allow various other engines to be fitted. The cowling behind the engine was made of aluminum that was engine-turned to provide an attractive scalloped effect that also covered blemishes created during the hand-forming process. Hawley Bowlus and Jon van der Linde carefully constructed the first M-1, and on February 14, 1926, Claude Ryan took it airborne for the first time.

Ryan's test flight revealed some problems in the design that were corrected by Jack Northrop, then an engineer for Donald Douglas. With Northrop's blessing the M-1 proved itself a rugged and dependable aircraft capable of lifting considerable loads for its size.

One month earlier in January 1926, Oregon bus line operator Vern Gorst had won the coveted Contract Air Mail Route #8 to carry airmail between Seattle and Los Angeles for his newly formed Pacific Air Transport. After surveying the route in an M-1, Gorst purchased six of the new Ryans and immediately put them to work. Later versions of the Ryan fitted with the Northrop-engineered I-beam spar wing were sold as M-2s and were acquired by other airmail contractors.

The *Spirit of St. Louis*'s design was based in part on the popular Ryan M-2 mail plane.

Nighttime flying in the cold Pacific winter months demonstrated a requirement for an enclosed cockpit version of the M-1/M-2. During the summer of 1926 Hawley Bowlus, Jack Northrop, and Walter Locke took the existing M-2 design and reengineered it to seat four inside the fuselage, with the pilot sitting in front just behind the engine and a baggage compartment behind the passenger section. The aircraft had a wingspan of thirty-six feet. A 200-horsepower Wright-Hispano drove a single two-bladed wooden propeller. Called the Bluebird for its dark blue wings and light blue fuselage, only one was built, which flew as a corporate aircraft until it was wrecked in a crash.

The Bluebird showed promise, but soon Ryan designer Ed Morrow drafted a larger iteration with a forty-two-foot wingspan to be known as the B-1 or "Brougham," to reflect luxury-car qualities. Realizing that the narrow landing gear

In order to train himself to fly the *Spirit of St. Louis*, Lindbergh flew the only Ryan Bluebird ever built.

The wider landing gear design of the Ryan Brougham was incorporated into the design of the *Spirit of St. Louis*. This configuration transmitted loads through the forward wing strut and into the main spar.

of the M-2 and Bluebird was too small to carry the greater weight of the B-1, Morrow designed a wider one that transmitted loads through the forward wing strut and into the main spar.

Meanwhile Claude Ryan and B. F. Mahoney grew increasingly at odds with one another. Ryan wished to expand their enterprise by taking the company public, while Mahoney was content with the status quo. Frustrated, Ryan sold his part of the company to Mahoney on November 30, 1926, thereby dissolving their partnership. Ryan later formed a new company that would bear his name, but his legal connection with his former partner and their firm was permanently severed. Claude Ryan did stay for a while as general manager, however, and for the moment Ryan Airlines continued to operate under its original name.

The Ryan factory employees gather in front of the newly-built *Spirit of St. Louis.*

With the Brougham taking shape in January 1927, Mahoney hired a new engineer from Douglas by the name of Donald Hall to work out the details of this new aircraft. Construction was just beginning on the prototype when Ryan received the telegram from a Charles Lindbergh of the Robertson Aircraft Corporation, St. Louis, Missouri, asking if his company could build an aircraft capable of crossing the Atlantic Ocean.

LINDBERGH ARRIVED IN SAN DIEGO ON FEBRUARY 23, 1927. The Ryan factory was set up in an unimposing old fish cannery by the waterfront. He was met by Mahoney, Hall, and office manager Walter Locke, and given a tour of the small facility, where he was introduced to the rest of the thirty-five-person staff. He was

not impressed. After the group settled the cost of the aircraft at $10,000, Lindbergh and Hall sat down to hash out the details. Quickly, it became apparent that Lindbergh had come to the right place. Hall and the rest of the crew were thoroughly professional and completely up to the daunting task ahead of them.

What Lindbergh wanted was a monoplane powered by a Wright J-5-C that would give him sufficient power reserve on takeoff. This was the latest model of this excellent engine and the first fitted with enclosed self-lubricating rocker arms and sodium-cooled exhaust valves. The aircraft was to have a 400-gallon fuel load distributed in fuselage and wing tanks. Lindbergh insisted that the pilot sit behind the main fuel tank to protect himself in case of an accident. He remembered too well the stories of his Army days when pilots of DH-4 light bombers were often crushed to death in forced landings, while their observers usually survived because the main fuel tank sat between them. Lindbergh's insistence that only he would fly the aircraft concerned Hall, but made the engineer's technical job easier, for with the two hundred pounds saved he could install tanks that could hold almost thirty extra gallons.

The fuel location was ideal for safety and for maintaining the aircraft's correct center of gravity. However, it was not ideal for visibility. Lindbergh was not in the least concerned for he believed, based on his two thousand hours of flight experience, that looking out the side windows and sideslipping the airplane when necessary would be sufficient. Airmail pilots could not see over the nose of their DH-4s during takeoff and, with

The *Spirit of St. Louis*'s engine is a Wright J-5-C Whirlwind.

the exception of flying low, where the danger of striking an obstacle was greatest, there was no need to see directly ahead, especially if flying over open stretches of water on instruments. Lindbergh's logic was sound, but former U.S. Navy submariner Charlie Randolph thought otherwise. Though employed to install the wing ribs, he designed and built an ingenious periscope that protruded out of the left side of the cockpit. To Lindbergh's surprise, it worked quite well and caused little extra drag. Nevertheless, Randolph designed it to retract when not in use, just like on a submarine.

The aircraft was to have a cruising speed of 100 miles per hour and a range of at least 4,000 miles. At first, neither Lindbergh nor Hall knew exactly how far New York was from Paris. A quick trip to the local library and carefully placed string on a globe revealed that the two cities were approximately 3,610 miles apart. The four hundred extra miles of range was to serve as a reserve in case Lindbergh was blown off course or encountered severe headwinds.

In order to save time and finish the *Spirit of St. Louis* in two months, Hall originally wanted to simply modify the existing M-2 design and incorporate other features from the Bluebird and Brougham as well. He quickly realized that this was not practical. While Hall used as many existing parts as he could, the new Ryan NY-P ended up as an original design.

Because of the tremendous weight of the fuel (2,750 pounds), Hall realized that the aircraft had to have a greater wingspan, longer fuselage, and a wider land-

Lindbergh had a special retractable periscope installed in the *Spirit* allowing him to see more clearly while flying at low altitudes. A lever on the instrument panel moved the periscope into position.

This scale model shows the construction of the wing and the location of three of the *Spirit*'s five fuel tanks.

ing gear than the M-2. Furthermore, the gross weight of the *Spirit* would have to be double the M-2's 2,500 pounds in order to carry the weight of the fuel.

The new wing used the same Clark Y airfoil as the M-2 and incorporated the excellent spruce and two-ply mahogany I-beam spar designed by Jack Northrop as well. The spar comprised four flanges glued to webs for added strength. At forty-six feet, the wing was ten feet longer than the M-2's, but Hall was able to preserve the same seven-foot chord. This increased the wing area 33 percent to 319 square feet and produced a wing loading of 16.7 pounds per square foot, resulting in a wing with sufficient range and take-off performance.

In order to ensure the accuracy of the airfoil shape, Hall placed the wing ribs eleven inches apart rather than fourteen or fifteen as was standard on the M-2. The wing ribs were built of spruce and constructed in a light and strong Warren truss design with double-piano-wire drag bracing and spruce compression members. He used plywood to conform more accurately around the leading edge of the wing. The wingtips were made of balsa and shaped to fit the airfoil for added streamlining.

In order not to overstress the lengthened wings, Hall designed ailerons 20 percent smaller than the M-2's and located thirty-eight inches from the wingtips. This was intended to reduce wingtip deflection under heavy loads for better aerodynamic efficiency. The wing was bolted on top of the fuselage and connected to the lower fuselage by two external struts. The struts were made of SAE 1020 mild carbon steel and streamlined with balsa wood.

Hall lengthened the fuselage to twenty-seven feet and eight inches, adding two feet in the tail and eighteen inches in the nose in order to preserve lateral stability. He moved the engine forward to preserve the balance of the aircraft. This allowed more room inside the fuselage for the twenty-five-gallon oil tank, which also served as a firewall, as well as an eighty-gallon nose fuel tank and a 200-gallon main fuel tank. Three fuel tanks totaling 145 gallons were placed inside the wings. This would allow fuel to feed the engine by gravity, should the fuel pump fail. The planned fuel load was 425 gallons, though Lindbergh's mechanics squeezed an extra twenty-five gallons into the *Spirit of St. Louis* before his transatlantic flight.

The tanks were built of soft sheet steel called ternplate, which would flex under strain but not leak. Fuel lines from all of the tanks fed into a central Lunkenheimer manifold below the instrument panel. By using a set of petcocks, Lindbergh could select which fuel tank he wanted to use. Fuel was moved through the system by a C-5 engine-driven pump to the carburetor. A hand-pump was also installed in case of emergency. At Lindbergh's insistence, the metal-tubed fuel lines were cut every eighteen inches and joined by flexible rubber fittings. Again based on his experience, he wished to minimize the risk of a fuel line breaking loose, caused by endless hours of vibration. Because of poor reliability, no gasoline gauge was installed. Instead, a sight gauge was attached to a half-gallon reserve tank to measure fuel consumption.

The fuselage itself was made of welded SAE 1020 mild carbon steel, as were the tail surfaces. The fuselage was also of Warren truss design that obviated the need for internal bracing wires. The engine mount was built separately and attached to the nose by four nickel steel bolts. Lindbergh sat in an enclosed fuselage with a removable celluloid window on each side and a celluloid skylight upon which was mounted his magnetic compass. A single door was installed on the right side of the cockpit. A wicker seat with a leather seat pad was bolted to the frame, while the cockpit floor was constructed of plywood. A conventional stick-and-rudder control system for flying the aircraft was installed with the rudder pedals. All of the general dimensions were designed to fit Lindbergh's lanky six-foot-three-inch, 165-pound frame.

Lindbergh also insisted on the latest instruments. Of course, he carried the standard instruments of his day, including an air speed indicator, an inclinometer—an early device to measure angle of attack—a drift meter, a stopwatch, a Jones

AERO DIGEST
CUTAWAY

FUEL TANK VENT

FLAME-PROOF FIREWALL

WELDED STEEL ENGINE MOUNT

OIL TANK - 27 GAL.

SPARK ADVANCE CONTROL

INTAKE MANIFOLD

EXHAUST STACK

WRIGHT J-5-C ENGINE

STANDARD STEEL
PROPELLER

PITOT HEAD

FUEL TANK-58 GAL.

TANK SUPPORT STRAP

THROTTLE CONTROL ROD

FUEL TANK-209 GAL.

PLYWOOD LEADING EDGE

WING ROOT FAIRING

FUEL TANK-86 GAL.

MAGNETO COOLING LOUVRES

CARBURETOR PRE-HEAT

TIRE VALVE ACCESS

RYAN NY-P

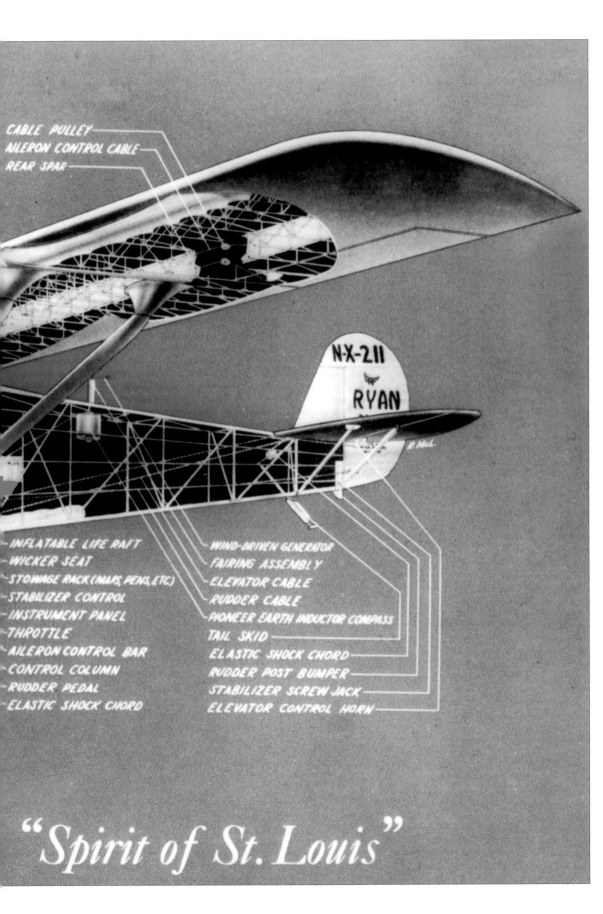

CABLE PULLEY
AILERON CONTROL CABLE
REAR SPAR

N·X-211
RYAN

R. McL.

- INFLATABLE LIFE RAFT
- WICKER SEAT
- STOWAGE RACK (MAPS, PENS, ETC.)
- STABILIZER CONTROL
- INSTRUMENT PANEL
- THROTTLE
- AILERON CONTROL BAR
- CONTROL COLUMN
- RUDDER PEDAL
- ELASTIC SHOCK CHORD

- WIND-DRIVEN GENERATOR
- FAIRING ASSEMBLY
- ELEVATOR CABLE
- RUDDER CABLE
- PIONEER EARTH INDUCTOR COMPASS
TAIL SKID
ELASTIC SHOCK CHORD
RUDDER POST BUMPER
STABILIZER SCREW JACK
ELEVATOR CONTROL HORN

"*Spirit of St. Louis*"

This detailed diagram of the *Spirit of St. Louis* appeared in *Aero Digest* magazine.

Left: Lindbergh's seat in the *Spirit of St. Louis* was made of wicker. The seat was originally outfitted with an inflatable cushion but it was stolen by a souvenir hunter at Le Bourget.

Opposite: The *Spirit of St. Louis*'s cockpit did not allow forward visibility so Lindbergh relied primarily upon his instruments, which were the most sophisticated available in 1927. Lindbergh counted and recorded the passing hours in pencil marks on the upper right hand corner of the instrument panel. As each hour passed he would turn one of the valves below the panel switching to a different one of the aircraft's five fuel tanks.

1. Mirror
2. Earth Inductor Compass, Pioneer, Inst. Co., Type 301B
3. Altimeter-Aviation Section, Signal Corps, U.S. Army, Type G, No. 2044, Neko, Newark, N.J.
4. Periscope
5. Magneto Switch, Splitdorf, Model A 232
6. Tachometer-Victometer, Joseph V. Jones, New York, U.S. Navy Type B (Consolidated Inst. Co.)
7. Turn-and-Bank Indicator, Pioneer Inst. Co.
8. Airspeed Indicator, Pioneer Inst. Co., Type/179499
9. Clock, Waltham
10. Oil pressure, War Stock
11. Fuel Pressure, U. S. Navy Type B
12. Oil Temp. Motometer-Type C, U.S. Air Service, Boyce
13. Inclinometer-Degrees, W.C. Rieker, Maker, Philadelphia (Pioneer Inst. Co.)

INSTRUMENT PANEL

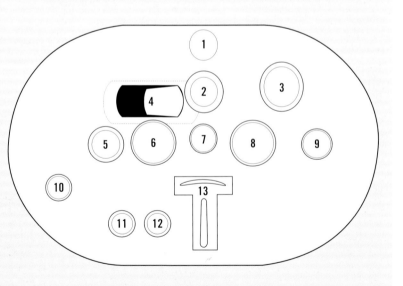

N.B.—*Information in parentheses taken from* Aviation, *June 20, 1927.*
Other information copied directly from instruments.

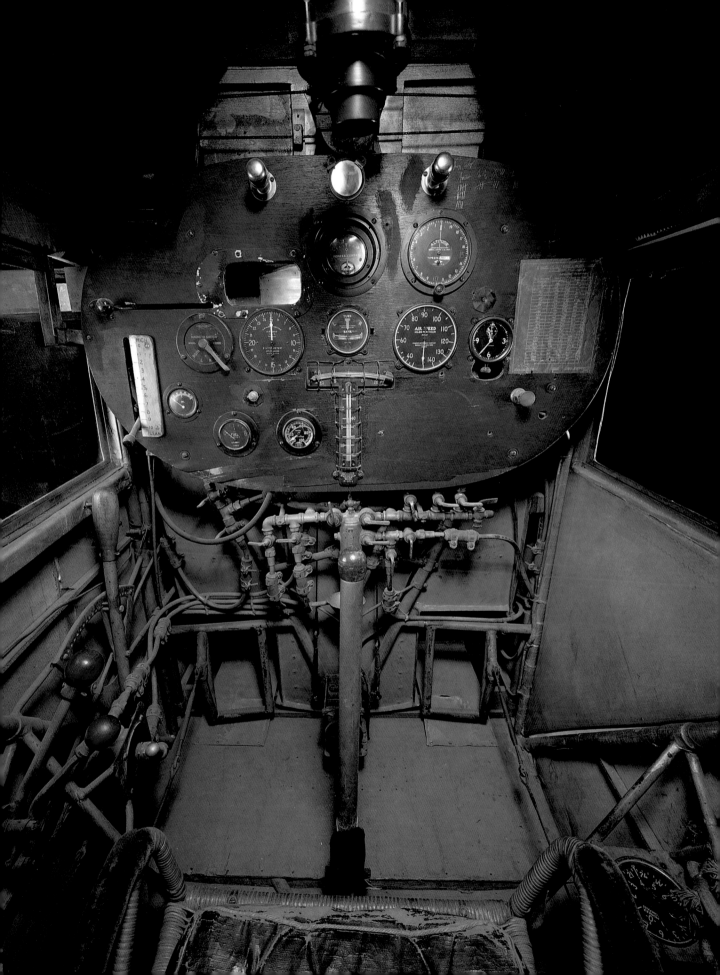

The earth inductor compass, now obsolete, was developed by scientists at the U.S. Bureau of Standards.

tachometer, an eight-day clock, an oil-pressure gauge, a "Motometer" that registered engine temperature, an altimeter, and an econometer that Lindbergh developed himself to determine fuel consumption efficiency. But he also wanted a turn-and-bank indicator that was just coming into general use, and a newly designed earth inductor compass. He had found the turn-and-bank indicator invaluable while flying his airmail routes at night and in fog, keeping him straight and level when his brain told him otherwise.

The earth inductor compass was thought to be more accurate than a conventional magnetic compass as it was less susceptible to inaccurate readings caused by acceleration, engine vibration, and three axis-of-movement forces within flying aircraft. This instrument, powered by an air-driven windmill generator mounted in the rear of the fuselage, would generate an electrical field that would be aligned with the earth's magnetic field. By turning the brushes inside the generator with a controller mounted in the cockpit, the alignment is changed and a new heading and course can be selected. An indicator mounted on the instrument panel keeps the aircraft on course: a needle will swing right or left of center if the pilot deviates from his flight path.

The instruments were mounted on a black-painted plywood panel, except for the magnetic compass, which was mounted on the skylight window frame away from metallic sources of interference. The Pioneer Instrument Company of Brooklyn, New York, manufactured the flight and navigation instruments. Although the instrument panel was lighted, Lindbergh later found the illumination too bright at night. Instead he preferred to fly with the luminescence of the radium-painted dials. Lindbergh's instruments were mildly radioactive, as were those in almost every aircraft of that time.

The horizontal and vertical tails, which were also constructed of SAE 1020 steel, were among the few parts taken directly from the M-2 design. Horizontal

The design of the tail of
the *Spirit of St. Louis* was
taken from the Ryan M-2.

trim could be changed in flight through a lever mounted on the left side of the cockpit that could raise or lower the stabilizer about an inch. Donald Hall was quite concerned that these surfaces were too small to control a heavy aircraft in flight. He wanted to build a proper empennage but did not have enough time. Lindbergh disagreed; he felt that the M-2 tail would reduce drag and increase range, which was all important. Though the aircraft would be more difficult to fly, Lindbergh reasoned that the extra effort in constantly having to fly a slightly unstable aircraft could actually help him stay alert. He was right, and it saved his life over the Atlantic.

The landing gear was derived from the design of the Bluebird and Brougham, which were wider and stronger than the M-2s. Built of high-strength chrome molybdenum steel—heat treated to withstand forces of 180,000 pounds per square inch—and designed to a load factor of four, the landing gear was a split axle hinged at the lower longeron of the fuselage. The shock absorbers were made of elastic cord and mounted inboard of the axle in a streamlined housing and connected vertically to the front wing strut. A strong triangle was formed by connecting this to structure the upper and lower longerons. The wheels were wire spoked and mounted B. F. Goodrich Silvertown thirty-by-four-inch tires. There were no brakes. A tailskid, standard for the day, was used instead.

The 223 horsepower Wright J-5-C Whirlwind mounted in the nose was the latest and best engine available. Made of aluminum and steel, the Whirlwind featured nine cylinders cooled by fins that protruded into the airstream, with an outside diameter of forty-five inches and length of thirty-four inches. With a bore of 4.5 inches and a stroke of 5.5 inches, the J-5-C had a displacement of 788 cubic inches and a compression ratio of 5.2 to 1. Its dry weight was 508 pounds. Wright guaranteed that the engine would consume no more than .60 and .025 pound per horsepower of gasoline and oil, respectively. Lindbergh's Whirlwind would soon well exceed its guarantee with exceptionally low fuel and oil consumption. A starter and a carburetor heater to prevent ice buildup were excluded to save weight.

Lindbergh's J-5-C was special. Previously, the Whirlwind had generally been used only by the military. With the rise of interest in the Orteig Prize and long-distance flight, several civilian orders were placed in February 1927. Word reached the shopfloor from management that, unlike the standard J-5, these engines were to be built with zero tolerance for the design specifications. Wright was assembling engines for Commander Richard Byrd, Lt. Commander Noel Davis, and Clarence Chamberlin, who was to fly the Bellanca that Lindbergh had wanted earlier.

Tom Rutledge was the youngest and newest engine builder at the Paterson, New Jersey, plant. Although he wanted to build Chamberlin's engine, he was assigned to build the Whirlwind for the obscure airmail pilot out in California that few believed could win the Orteig Prize. Despite his youth, Rutledge carefully assembled the special engine, completing the task in April. As events would demonstrate, Tom Rutledge knew his craft.

Another state-of-the-art item Lindbergh selected was an all-metal propeller. Concerned with the possibility of failure that was commonplace with contemporary propellers, Lindbergh and Hall chose a two-bladed propeller of duralumin built by the Standard Steel Propeller Company of Pittsburgh, Pennsylvania. Originally developed at McCook Field for the U.S. Army by MIT graduate Frank Caldwell, this propeller was strong, lightweight, and durable. Working with Standard, Caldwell developed a revolutionary propeller that obviated the need for designing specific propellers for specific engines, as was common practice.

By installing propeller blades that could be adjusted before flight to suit the power and performance characteristics of the aircraft and engine, Standard could cut production costs by building a propeller system that was suitable for many different applications. Furthermore, the blades could be adjusted to a fine pitch to extract the maximum power from the aircraft, or adjusted for coarse pitch to maximize efficiency in cruise. Lindbergh understandably chose a coarse 16.25-degree setting on his two-bladed propeller to squeeze the most miles from his engine and fuel. It would make for a very long take-off run, especially when fully loaded. This was a chance he was willing to take.

The entire aircraft was covered in Flightex brand Grade A Arizona Pima cotton coated with six coats of aluminum pigmented dope. Careful attention was paid to streamlining the entire aircraft with fairings around the wing roots and where the cowling met the leading edge of the wing. The cowling itself was hand-hammered from sheets of duralumin by Fred Rohr to fit carefully around the nose. The spinner and the spinner shroud were made the same way. Rohr expertly burnished the aluminum, also known as engine-turning, to produce the attractive signature scalloped swirls that were a trademark of Ryan metalworking. This also hid the blemishes of hand-formed sheet metal.

When completed, the Ryan NY-P *Spirit of St. Louis* carried a useful load of 2,985 pounds, including the pilot, and had a gross weight of 5,135 pounds. In fact, the *Spirit* carried 5,250 pounds when it left for Paris. The wing loading at gross weight was 16.10 pounds per square foot, light by today's standards, but consider-

able for the state of the art in 1927. Flight tests revealed a top speed of 124 miles per hour—four miles per hour faster than originally calculated—with an economical cruise speed of ninety-seven miles per hour fully loaded and sixty-seven miles per hour when lightly loaded. The still air range was estimated to be 4,110 statute miles.

The actual construction of the *Spirit* began in rather tense circumstances. Many employees resented the constant presence of Lindbergh in the factory, curtly overseeing every aspect of the design and construction. He was a stickler for perfection, demanding tolerances as close as a thirty-second of an inch. Soon, however, Lindbergh's enthusiasm and complete dedication to the job inspired the entire organization. John van der Linde, the chief mechanic, and Red Harrigan, the chief pilot, were impressed with Lindbergh's flying skills when "Slim" practiced in the company's M-2 and Bluebird to learn the idiosyncrasies of Ryan's monoplanes. At other times Lindbergh studied navigation, acquiring the Mercator projection charts necessary to plot a great circle route across the North Atlantic, as well as the indispensable Rand McNally railroad maps of the United States. He chose not to steer by the stars at night for he felt that he could not use a sextant and fly his unsteady aircraft at the same time. He would use dead reckoning to navigate, following his compasses hopefully to a landfall in Ireland and then on to Paris.

While safety was paramount to Lindbergh, so was weight, as every ounce saved allowed him that much more time in the air if he became lost. He chose to carry a rubber life raft, four red flares, an air-cushion seat, five cans of army rations, cord, a needle, fishing line and two hooks, a hacksaw blade, matches, a four-quart canteen of emergency water, a hunting knife, and a flashlight. He selected a wool flight suit—which would keep him warm when wet if he were forced down in the ocean—rather than cotton or leather. He also carried an Armburst cup that could gather drinking water from a person's breath. Lindbergh chose not to carry a heavy radio or a parachute, both of which were of little utility over the open ocean.

By April 1, with the fuselage built, it seemed inevitable that the *Spirit* would not be finished in time. Ryan and Mahoney placed the factory on overtime with everyone working into the night seven days a week. Though the crew was exhausted—at one point Donald Hall worked thirty-six hours straight—they had become true believers in the project and rushed the aircraft to completion. Two weeks later the main fuel tank was installed with only an eighth of an inch to spare. With Lindbergh critiquing every step and demanding last-minute changes, the aircraft quickly came together. In a gesture of esprit, the workers signed their names to the

Opposite:
The *Spirit*'s special, hand-built Wright J-5-C Whirlwind engine powered a two-bladed Standard duralumin propeller. The aluminum cowling was burnished to create an attractive finish. The nose of the *Spirit* was painted to display the flags of those countries Lindbergh visited while flying the plane.

The inside of the original spinner cap was painted with the names of all the people who built the *Spirit of St. Louis*. The figure in the center is a swastika, a Native American good luck symbol, which in 1927 retained its positive associations in the United States.

main spar. Later, their names were also painted inside the spinner cap, albeit with several misspellings.

The news of April 27 that Davis and Wooster, two of Lindbergh's competitors, had perished in the crash of their Keystone Pathfinder *American Legion*, equipped with three Wright J-5 Whirlwind engines, underscored the seriousness of their efforts. Byrd, they knew, had also damaged his aircraft. The following day, two months to the day after the contract had been finalized, the Ryan NY-P *Spirit of St. Louis* was finished. It had taken the entire thirty-five-member workforce of Ryan Airlines two months with 775 hours of Donald Hall's engineering time and three thousand hours of shop time to build the aircraft.

The *Spirit* leaves San Diego for a test flight.

John van der Linde refuels the *Spirit* using a funnel. On the ground stand (left to right) O. R. McNeel, welding foreman; George Hammond, student mechanic pilot; Charles Lindbergh; Donald Hall, chief engineer; and A. J. Edwards.

Six days earlier, Major Clarence Young, a friend of Lindbergh's and now the chief of the air regulations division of the aeronautics branch of the Department of Commerce had arrived in San Diego with the paperwork certifying the aircraft for experimental flight. The department had assigned the *Spirit* the designation N-X-211: "N" was the internationally recognized aviation symbol for the United States while "X" reflected the aircraft's experimental status. That meant Lindbergh was not permitted to take along any paying passengers, not that he was planning to do so.

Before the new Ryan could be flown, the aircraft had to be moved out of the factory. Unfortunately, with the *Spirit*'s forty-six-foot wingspan it would not fit down the steps from its second-floor assembly area. Cleverly, the crew removed the doors to the top floor, moved a nearby boxcar on railroad tracks underneath the opening and took the wing out and onto the box car and then to the ground without incident. Soon the aircraft was assembled on Dutch Flats, and on April 28, John van der Linde pulled the Standard propeller through and started the Whirlwind on its first try. Assistant mechanic Douglas Corrigan, famously nicknamed "Wrong Way" Corrigan for an incident that occurred when he flew across the Atlantic himself eleven years later, removed the wheel chocks. Quickly the *Spirit* was airborne.

To everyone's delight the aircraft flew beautifully. Lindbergh was impressed with its speed and power when it was lightly loaded. So pleased was he that on this first flight he even performed a mock dogfight with a Navy Curtiss Hawk fighter from nearby North Island. The aircraft was indeed moderately unstable but it was nothing Lindbergh could not handle. Generally speaking, the controls were well coordinated and the stall quite predictable. Subsequent tests at Camp Kearney verified the aircraft's ability to fly heavily loaded. Unfortunately, Lindbergh himself was unable to test the aircraft fully loaded. After the test flight with 300 gallons of fuel on board, the aircraft wheel bearings overheated and the tailskid broke. Lindbergh decided that he could not risk test-flying the *Spirit* again with the burden of additional fuel. The aircraft was now ready for the first leg of its attempted flight across the Atlantic.

The Flight

ON MAY 10, 1927, Lindbergh bade Ryan Airlines farewell and headed east in the *Spirit of St. Louis*, first to St. Louis and then to New York for his final preparations. He almost did not make it. The Wright Aeronautical Corporation's engineers had assured him that because of the higher quality of California gasoline there would be no problem with carburetor icing. They were wrong. Lindbergh had taken off with half-full tanks and was looking forward to getting used to his new machine on its first long-distance flight. He was flying mostly at night and relying on his earth inductor compass. All was well until he reached the Rocky Mountains somewhere in New Mexico. He climbed to above 10,000 feet when suddenly the engine began to cough. Thinking quickly, he applied more power, which ameliorated the sputtering but did not cure it. Lindbergh sweated out some very tense minutes before the engine began to run more smoothly in the warmer air of the Great Plains. He vowed then and there to install a carburetor heater box regardless of the weight, because the air over the North Atlantic would be colder and moister than the Rockies and much more prone to forming ice.

Lindbergh had earlier made arrangements to purchase five hundred gallons of Standard Oil's finest California gasoline to be shipped to New York. The Vacuum Oil Company, providers of the Mobiloil for the *Spirit*, agreed to handle the fuel and oil for Lindbergh for free in New York. At that time gasoline refining was still in its early stages and industrial chemists as yet did not fully understand the energy content of fuels or how to control engine knocking caused by preignition. What they did know was that gasoline refined from California petroleum had a higher energy content than gasoline from other areas. Today this fuel is described as having a higher octane rating.

The rest of the flight to St. Louis was uneventful, and Lindbergh was warmly welcomed by his backers when he landed there. After a brief rest, he flew to Curtiss

Opposite:
Lindbergh leans out of one of the two side windows of his Ryan aircraft. The design of the *Spirit of St. Louis* did not include a forward-facing window.

Field in Garden City, Long Island, where he arrived on May 12 after setting a transcontinental speed record of twenty-one hours and twenty minutes. The leg from San Diego to St. Louis was the longest anyone had ever flown by themselves.

Lindbergh was greeted on Long Island by famous Curtiss test pilot and then airport manager, Casey Jones. Expecting to have to find his own hangar space and mechanic, Lindbergh found that Casey had already assigned him his own hangar. Wright Aeronautical representative Dick Blythe catered to Lindbergh's needs and provided him with their best technicians, including field-service representative Ken Boedecker and mechanic Ed Mulligan. Brice Goldsborough from the Pioneer Instrument Company also offered his services, along with a new earth inductor compass. With Blythe handling all of the public relations details, Lindbergh was free to prepare for the flight while suffering through endless photo opportunities with the ever-invasive press. Lindbergh's record-setting transcontinental flight had gained much attention; he was now seen as a solid contender.

The *Spirit* is rolled out of its hangar at Curtiss Field for a test flight on May 14, 1927.

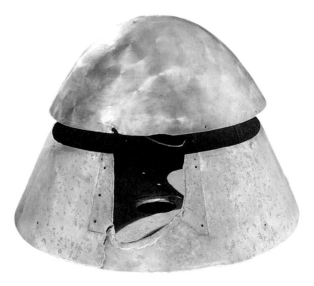

It was discovered that
the *Spirit of St. Louis*'s
original spinner shroud
had cracked during
Lindbergh's flight from
California to New York.
The crack is evident in
the center of the shroud.
A new shroud and cap
were fabricated prior to
Lindbergh's journey
to Paris.

Much work was still to be done while Lindbergh and the other contenders waited for good weather. At Curtiss Field, Wright mechanics installed the much-needed carburetor heater box. Lindbergh had the six dry-cell batteries that powered the instrument panel lights removed. The lights were too bright. Instead, he would use his flashlight and save a few more precious pounds of weight.

Meanwhile, mechanic Ed Mulligan had discovered that a severe crack had developed in the *Spirit*'s spinner shroud. On his own initiative Mulligan removed the spinner cap, the propeller, and the shroud and arranged with Curtiss to fabricate a new cap and shroud at no cost.

Lindbergh was overwhelmed by the camaraderie and generosity of everyone inspired by the Orteig competition. An unknown doctor gave Lindbergh a first-aid kit and sunglasses and a little girl, also unknown to Lindbergh, gave him a mirror so he could place it on his instrument panel and read his magnetic compass, which was designed to be read backward. Furthermore, Richard Byrd, one of Lindbergh's most serious competitors, offered him the use of nearby Roosevelt Field, which he had leased, with its longer cinder runway. This astonished Lindbergh.

Lindbergh was equally impressed by the enthusiasm and support of his financial backers. The rules of the Orteig competition required that the entry form be submitted sixty days before takeoff. The sixty days had not elapsed and Lindbergh was concerned that if he took off beforehand he would not win the $25,000 even if he completed the flight. A quick telephone call to Harry Knight assuaged his fear. "To hell with the money," Lindbergh remembered him saying. Knight told him to take off whenever he was ready.

Following spread:
Lindbergh's test flights
with the *Spirit* typically
attracted a crowd of
interested observers,
as pictured here at
Curtiss Field.

The competitors for the Orteig Prize seen here meeting the press at Mitchel Field, Long Island, included Lindbergh (left), the well-known Arctic explorer Richard E. Byrd (center), and leading American pilot Clarence Chamberlin (right). On June 4, 1927, well after Lindbergh had succeeded in winning the Orteig Prize, Chamberlin and his sponsor Charles Levine set out for Berlin in their Bellanca *Columbia* but were forced to land in Eisleben, Germany. Byrd and his crew took off for Paris on June 29, in their Fokker *America,* but crash landed in the ocean south of Le Havre, short of their destination.

Opposite: Lindbergh was awarded the $25,000 Orteig Prize even though he left for Paris less than sixty days after his entry form, reproduced here, was submitted.

Feb. 26, 1927

The Raymond Orteig $25,000 Prize

PARIS - NEW YORK —— NEW YORK - PARIS
Trans-Atlantic Flight

(Under the rules of the Fédération Aéronautique Internationale of Paris, France, and National Aeronautic Association of the United States of America of Washington, D. C.)

ENTRY FORM

Name of Aviator Entrant (in full) ___Charles A. Lindbergh,___

Address ___% Mr. H. H. Knight, 401 Olive St., St. Louis, Missouri.___

Aviator's F. A. I. Certificate No. ___6286___ Issued by ___National Aeronautic Ass'n.,___

Aviator's Annual License No. ___295 (1927)___ Issued by ___National Aeronautic Ass'n.,___

PARTICULARS RELATING TO THE AIRCRAFT INTENDED TO BE USED.

Type, (Monoplane, Biplane, Hydroaeroplane, Flying Boat, etc.) *NYP Ryan Monoplane*

Wing area in sq. ft. *290* Load per sq. ft. *15½ lb*

Make and type of engine *Wright J5 "whirlwind"* Cu. in. Disp.

Approximate capacity of Fuel Tanks *425 gallons*

I, the undersigned, ___Charles A. Lindbergh,___

of ___% Mr. H. H. Knight, 401 Olive St., St. Louis, Mo.,___ hereby enter for the Raymond Orteig "New York-Paris" $25,000 Prize upon the following conditions:—

1. I agree to observe and abide by the Rules and Regulations for the time being in force and governing the contest, and to comply in all respects and at all times with the requests or instructions regarding the contest, which may be given to me by any of the Officials of the National Aeronautic Association of the United States of America.

2. In addition to, and not by the way of, limitation of the liabilities assumed by me by this entry under the said Rules and Regulations, I agree also to indemnify the National Aeronautic Association of the United States of America and the Trustees of the Raymond Orteig $25,000 Prize, and Mr. Raymond Orteig, the donor of the New York-Paris Flight Prize, or their representatives or servants, or any fellow competitor, against all claims and damages arising out of, or caused by, any ascent, flight or descent made by me whether or not such claims and demands shall arise directly out of my own actions or out of the acts, actions or proceedings of any persons assembling to witness or be present at such ascent or descent.

3. I enclose my certified check for $250.00 to the order of the Trustees of the Raymond Orteig $25,000 Prize, being Entrance Fee, and request to be entered on the Competitors' Register of the National Aeronautic Association of the United States of America.

Signature *Charles A. Lindbergh*

(Notary Seal.)

Address *% Mr. Harry H. Knight*

Subscribed and sworn to before me this 15th day of Feb. 1927. *401 Olive St.*

Date Feb. 15, 1927 *St. Louis Mo.*

My commission expires *May 9 1927*

This blank is to be executed and forwarded with certified check to The Contest Committee of the National Aeronautic Association at No. 1623 H Street, Washington, D. C., and notice thereof immediately communicated to

The Secretary of the Trustees of the
Raymond Orteig Twenty-Five Thousand Dollar Prize
c/o Army and Navy Club of America

During the wait, thousands of New Yorkers dropped by to visit all of the participants. The seeds of Lindbergh's lifelong animosity toward the press were planted now. Journalists fabricated stories about him and interfered with his preparations. On one occasion Lindbergh broke his tailskid when he had to veer away from a photographer who stood in his way as he landed. The many stories so concerned his mother that she took a train from Detroit and spent a day with him just to make sure he was all right.

Charles Lawrance, the creator of the Wright Whirlwind-series engines CK, dropped by, as did many dignitaries, including René Fonck, Al Williams, Anthony Fokker, Chance Vought, Harry Guggenheim, and the head of the Curtiss corporation, Clement Keys. B. F. Mahoney arrived later from San Diego. On a visit to Theodore Roosevelt, Jr., Lindbergh received letters of introduction to the U.S. Ambassador to France, Myron T. Herrick. These and letters from the Springfield, Illinois, postmaster William H. Conkling and airmail buddy George Brandenweide were all the mail that Lindbergh would carry.

By the end of the week, Lindbergh was eager for a favorable weather report from meteorologist James H. Kimball. When another day passed with an unfavorable forecast, Lindbergh accepted an invitation to see a show in Manhattan. On his way to see *Rio Rita* with Blythe and others, he stopped the car on 42nd Street to

check with Kimball one more time. Kimball was now forecasting clearing skies over the Atlantic. Although he had been awake all day and the previous night, Lindbergh canceled his night out and returned to Curtiss Field to prepare for his departure.

On the way back, Lindbergh picked up six sandwiches for the flight. With his team hard at work, he returned to his hotel to attempt to sleep. Between the excitement and an interruption from a well-meaning friend, it was useless. Just before three in the morning, he arrived at his hangar at Curtiss Field. To his pleasant surprise, he learned that Ken Lane, the chief engineer for the Wright Aeronautical Corporation, had made arrangements for the *Spirit* to be towed by truck next door to Roosevelt Field, so it would not have to be flown there. At Roosevelt Field the mechanics carefully loaded 450 gallons of Standard Oil's finest California gasoline into the Ryan. They decided that twenty gallons of oil, not twenty-five, would be sufficient. The specially assembled Wright had consumed considerably less oil than expected on its transcontinental flight, a testament to its makers. With a small sealed barograph now on board to document the flight officially, Lindbergh was ready to go.

Taking off was a great concern. The field was still soaked and muddy from the rain. During the time it took to refuel, the wind had changed and was now blowing five miles per hour behind Lindbergh. Most important, the *Spirit* was heavily

A truck tows the *Spirit* from Curtiss Field to Roosevelt Field in the early morning hours of May 20, 1927.

laden with fuel, tipping the scales at 5,250 pounds—the heaviest it had ever been or would be.

Aware of the difficulties, Lindbergh pressed on. The dependable Whirlwind engine fired up quickly, but idled three hundred revolutions lower than normal. While the mechanic assured Lindbergh that this was caused by the dawn's dampness, it was one more thing to worry about. Undaunted, Lindbergh fastened his seat belt, pulled down his goggles, advanced the throttle, and slowly began to move. In what seemed like ages, the *Spirit* gradually gained momentum as it bounced through puddles on the uneven ground. Gradually Lindbergh began to feel the air pressure on his controls and gingerly lifted off, clearing the telephone poles at the end of the field by no more than twenty feet. It was 7:54 A.M. Eastern Daylight Time.

FOR A WHILE THE *SPIRIT* WAS ESCORTED by other aircraft. Remaining at 150 feet in "ground effect" while slowly burning off fuel, Lindbergh used his periscope to make sure his route was clear of obstacles. Every fifteen minutes he switched to another fuel tank to make sure that none of them overflowed. Soon the weather cleared.

The next thirty-three and a half hours established a routine. Every hour Lindbergh would switch to another fuel tank and mark that fact in pencil on the upper right side of his instrument panel. Also every hour he would adjust his magnetic and earth inductor compasses to compensate for the changes in the earth's magnetic field. After crossing Massachusetts he took out his Mercator chart and began to fly a great circle route toward Nova Scotia and beyond. Although Lindbergh had brought sandwiches and a one-quart canteen of water with him, he would consume little, believing that hunger pangs would help him stay awake. After several hours his body started to cramp up from the confined quarters, but eventually the pain subsided, as he knew it would. All the while, the Wright engine droned steadily on.

After nine hours of flying, the urge to sleep started to overcome Lindbergh. The struggle to stay awake would dominate Lindbergh's efforts until he crossed the Irish coast. Time and again he would drift off, only to catch himself when his unstable aircraft would fall away on one wing and force him to reawaken. As night fell, thirteen hours after his take-off, Lindbergh increased his altitude and flew using only his main and nose fuel tanks, keeping the wing tanks in reserve and changing the pitch of his stabilizer to compensate for the lessening fuel load. By this time he was flying only on instruments and often in clouds, with the eerie glow of the radium dials and the occasional light of his flashlight to guide him. His life was now

Right: The *Spirit of St. Louis* was equipped with a sealed barograph so Lindbergh could substantiate his transatlantic flight. The instrument was installed by Carl Schory of the National Aeronautic Association.

Below: The barograph recorded the altitude and the duration of Lindbergh's flight on a slowly revolving paper covered cylinder.

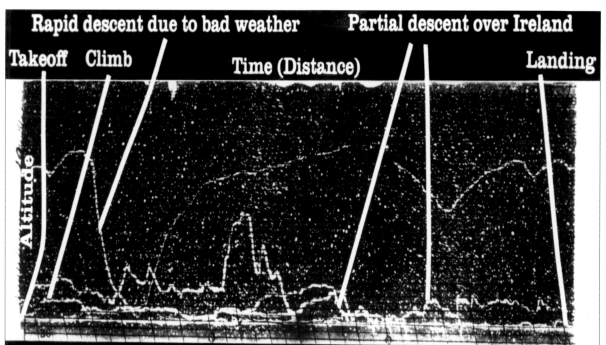

Rapid descent due to bad weather   Partial descent over Ireland

Takeoff   Climb   Time (Distance)   Landing

Altitude

This is the barograph record of the "Spirit of St. Louis" transatlantic flight. Because the flight lasted about 33½ hours and the drum revolved every 6 hours, the continuous tracing occupies more than 5 lines.

In the early morning hours of May 20, 1927, Lindbergh suits-up just before taking off for Paris.

in the hands of his turn-and-bank indicator, which kept him straight and level when he could not see.

Many more dangers awaited him. After fourteen hours in the air, Lindbergh was calmly cruising in clouds at 10,500 feet when the *Spirit* began to ice up. Fearing that his flight instruments might freeze, Lindbergh carefully turned and descended to look for warmer air. All the way he fought the overwhelming urge to turn quickly for he could easily lose control in the dark. After ten minutes, he found his way out of the thunderhead and into clear air.

Fifteen hours into the flight, Lindbergh's two compasses failed him. While he was somewhat skeptical of the new earth inductor compass, Lindbergh had faith in his standard magnetic compass, but now it began to swing wildly in ninety-degree arcs. While he had heard stories of magnetic storms, most pilots rejected these tales. Now Lindbergh was forced to confront this unknown phenomenon. Fortunately for him, the compass slowly stabilized and eventually returned to normal. Unfortunately, Lindbergh no longer knew if he was still on course. Intuitively he determined from the position of the rising moon and from studying his charts that he was at least close to his planned route.

Halfway through the flight, fatigue was Lindbergh's most dangerous adversary. He fought back with every trick he knew: he left the side windows out in order to keep the flow of cold air on his face, and he studied his Mercator chart to refocus his mind on his navigation duties. Increasingly the *Spirit* would wake him up as it fell away when he began to doze off. Lindbergh struggled to maintain his hourly routine of resetting his compasses to stay on course and switching fuel tanks. Numb with exhaustion, he began to lose track of time and found himself in a state of what he called "eye-open sleep." He was so tired that at one point he began to see apparitions in the rear of the fuselage. Only the fear of death enabled him to fight off his exhaustion.

At daybreak, twenty hours after he had lifted off from Roosevelt Field, Lindbergh realized that he was winning his battle. Having survived the night, he now descended to 1,500 feet. His air-filled seat cushion now deflated in the denser air and Lindbergh kept to his routine, cruising at one hundred miles per hour at 1,650 rpm. At one point he rummaged through his flight suit and discovered a St. Christopher medal that an unknown person had slipped into his pocket while in New York. Now in the sunshine, he contemplated wearing sunglasses but decided against it, believing that they would be too comfortable. By this time discomfort was an ally in his struggle to stay alert. Smelling salts did not work.

In the twenty-seventh hour, Lindbergh spotted a seagull and knew that land was near. Soon he flew over a fishing boat and naively tried to shout for directions to Ireland over the din of his engine. His attempt failed. Lindbergh need not have worried. Despite his fatigue, the hours of instrument flying, and the uncertainty of unknown crosswinds and swinging compasses, Lindbergh crossed the Irish coast only three miles from his estimated landfall; a truly remarkable feat of piloting. He was two and a half hours ahead of schedule and wide-awake at last. In his exuberance Lindbergh circled over Ireland and found himself following his earth inductor compass back out to sea, 180 degrees in the wrong direction. He quickly caught his error and, regaining his sense of direction, flew on to England, into the night, and finally to Paris, where a new world awaited him.

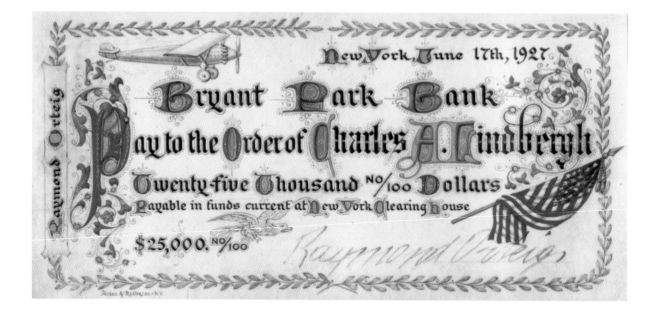

New York, June 17th, 1927

Bryant Park Bank

Pay to the Order of Charles A. Lindbergh

Twenty-five Thousand NO/100 Dollars

Payable in funds current at New York Clearing House

$25,000. NO/100

Raymond Orteig

The Orteig Prize of $25,000 was awarded to Charles A. Lindbergh for being the first person to fly nonstop from New York to Paris.

AFTER THE DELIRIOUS CROWD AT LE BOURGET carried Lindbergh away, the French air force rescued the *Spirit of St. Louis* from the mob of souvenir hunters and pulled it into a nearby hangar. There, mechanics replaced the fuselage fabric and repaired tears in the tail. They also replaced a rocker arm cover that had been stolen off the engine. When the mechanics checked the aircraft they discovered that it had eighty-five gallons of fuel left, enough for Lindbergh to have flown another 1,040 miles. Furthermore, the expertly built Whirlwind had only consumed five gallons of oil.

Lindbergh had expected to spend a few quiet days flying with French aviators before moving on. He had wildly underestimated the effect of his flight on the public's imagination. Now he was a hero to millions around the world and a celebrity of unmatched proportions. He also won the Orteig prize after all. A delighted Raymond Orteig set aside the sixty-day entry rule and happily announced that Lindbergh had won the cherished award.

After being feted in Paris, Lindbergh flew on to Belgium and London, where he was greeted by throngs of admirers. Before his transatlantic flight, he had not worked out how he would return to the United States if he succeeded. President Calvin Coolidge made this a moot point; he sent the cruiser USS *Memphis* to retrieve America's greatest pilot and the *Spirit of St. Louis*. In mid-June 1927, Lindbergh and his aircraft returned home, sailing up the Potomac River to

Lindbergh is warmly received at Paris's town hall after his successful transatlantic flight.

Beginning their journey
to Brussels, Belgium,
Lindbergh and the *Spirit*
fly south over Paris above
the Cours de la Reine.

A French mechanic
replenishes the *Spirit*'s
oil supply while in the
hangar at Le Bourget.

Lindbergh, in the cockpit,
prepares to leave Paris
for Brussels.

The *Spirit* warms up before leaving Le Bourget for Brussels.

Lindbergh arrives at London's
crowded Croydon airfield.

Lindbergh stands before the *Spirit* at the Washington Navy Yard following his return to the United States on the U.S.S. *Memphis* in June 1927.

Washington, D.C., to a hero's welcome. Similar celebrations greeted Lindbergh in New York, St. Louis, and in Ottawa, where he visited as the guest of the Canadian Prime Minister, W. L. Mackenzie King.

During the summer of 1927, Lindbergh prepared his personal recollections of his Atlantic flight, entitled *We* in reference to his almost spiritual connection to his aircraft. *We* immediately became a best-seller. Lindbergh wrote the manuscript while staying at the Long Island residence of philanthropist Harry Guggenheim, who was also the president of the influential Daniel Guggenheim Fund for the Promotion of Aeronautics. This fund provided crucial financial support for the development of the airline industry and aircraft safety. Guggenheim had visited Lindbergh at Curtiss Field and extended an invitation to meet after the flight. Lindbergh accepted, and between them they decided that a three-month aerial tour of the United States by Lindbergh in the *Spirit* would greatly increase the public's awareness of aviation and stimulate the use of airmail and commercial flight.

With support from the Guggenheim Fund and the cooperation of the Department of Commerce, Lindbergh carefully organized the expedition. William

P. MacCracken, the assistant secretary of the aeronautics branch of the Department of Commerce, provided a support aircraft piloted by Lindbergh's army buddy Philip R. Love and carrying Theodore R. Sorenson, a Wright mechanic, and Donald E. Keyhoe, from the Commerce Department, as Lindbergh's aide. C. C. Maidment would later replace Sorenson. Milburn Kusterer was sent ahead by train as the tour's advance representative.

On July 20, 1927, the tour began. After the completion of thorough maintenance, including the replacement of the faulty original clock, the *Spirit* left Mitchel Field, Long Island, and headed north to New England and then west into the Plains and up to the Northwest. From Seattle the tour flew south along the Pacific coast to San Diego, where Lindbergh received an especially heartfelt welcome from the city that built his aircraft. From there the tour turned eastwards, through the desert into Texas and the South, before heading north once again, ending the flight where it had started, at Mitchel Field, on October 23. The tour covered 22,350 miles and stopped in eighty-two cities. Lindbergh made a point of landing at least once in each of the then-forty-eight states. Each city was notified well in advance so that local authorities could plan the requisite parades and banquets before the tour moved on. Lindbergh insisted that he arrive at each destination at precisely 2:00 P.M. in order to demonstrate the efficiency and punctuality of civil flight. In fact, Lindbergh arrived on time everywhere except Portland, Maine, where he was delayed by fog.

Although Lindbergh insisted that the tour's purpose was only to promote aviation, it was clear to all that it had far greater significance. Millions turned out at every stop to catch a glimpse of America's greatest flying hero and to hear his message in countless speeches. Nevertheless, Lindbergh achieved his stated goal. Airfields were built throughout the nation in response to his visits as the public in general, and professional investors in particular, took a more serious interest in investing in aviation. The reliability of his aircraft and the punctuality of the tour underscored the im-

Lindbergh's forty-eight-state tour of the U.S. was sponsored by the Daniel Guggenheim Fund for the Promotion of Aeronautics. The tour's participants from left to right were Donald E. Keyhoe, Philip Love, Lindbergh, C. C. Maidment and Milburn Kusterer.

Donald Keyhoe shot this in-flight photograph of the *Spirit* during the U.S. tour.

mense strides aviation had made. With extra louvers cut into the aluminum cowling to improve cooling during the hot summer months, the *Spirit* performed flawlessly. In Minnesota the original thin tires were replaced by wider balloon tires to help the *Spirit* through the mud of the Midwest. Little else was changed. Only routine servicing was performed.

After the tour, Lindbergh's engine was disassembled and inspected. Having flown for over 355 hours, the Wright J-5-C Whirlwind No. 7331 exhibited only normal signs of wear. Earlier, when the *Spirit* had returned to the U.S. after its transatlantic flight, mechanics found fourteen pushrods that were slightly bent, two small cracks near the edge of the babbit in the upper half of the master rod bearing, slightly rusty exhaust valves, and slightly worn exhaust valve guides. Now, mechanics found very little else that needed attention. All of the valves, as well as the pistons, were in excellent condition. Some enamel paint had flaked off the cooling fins around the exhaust ports and slight pitting was noticed around the valve seats. The thrust bearing was binding. Mechanics reground all of the engine's valves, washed out the thrust ball bearing, and polished the compression rings. The engine was quickly reassembled and reinstalled in the *Spirit of St. Louis,* for Lindbergh had one more major flight to perform.

After the completion of the U.S. tour, Lindbergh had met with Dwight Morrow, a personal friend of President Calvin Coolidge and the recent chairman of the Morrow Board that the president had commissioned to examine the state of aeronautics in the United States. Morrow was also the U.S. ambassador to Mexico. During their discussion, Ambassador Morrow invited Lindbergh to visit Mexico as a symbol of goodwill, and also to emphasize the growing importance of civil aviation throughout the continent. Lindbergh readily agreed and decided that a direct flight between the two capitals would have the greatest political effect.

Lindbergh plotted out the 2,100-mile route between Washington, D.C., and Mexico City and, on December 13, 1927, took off from Bolling Field on the eastern shore of the Potomac River and headed toward Valbuena Airport. In what should have been an uneventful flight, despite the unpredictable December weather, Lindbergh flew a steady course until he was well over Mexico in clear air and in bright sunshine. Despite the fact that he had a new, more accurate altimeter installed in the aircraft, he was lost after having turned in the wrong direction while conducting a course correction. After scouring the countryside, he spotted the city of Toluca and realized he had missed his target by thirty-five miles. Sheepishly, he turned around and found Valbuena Airport, arriving two hours late, to the relief of Morrow and the president of Mexico, Plutarco Calles, who were anxiously waiting. This flight covered 2,100 miles in twenty-seven hours and fifteen minutes.

Lindbergh's visit was immensely successful. After a two-week visit, he pressed on into Central America to demonstrate the potential for regular, scheduled air service in this rugged land. Carrying a rifle, emergency rations, and a first-aid kit,

During daylight hours Lindbergh preferred to fly low in "ground effect" to take advantage of what he and other early aviators believed was a thicker cushion of air that improved an aircraft's performance. This photograph, demonstrating flying in ground effect, was taken over Yellowstone Lake in Wyoming during the U.S. tour.

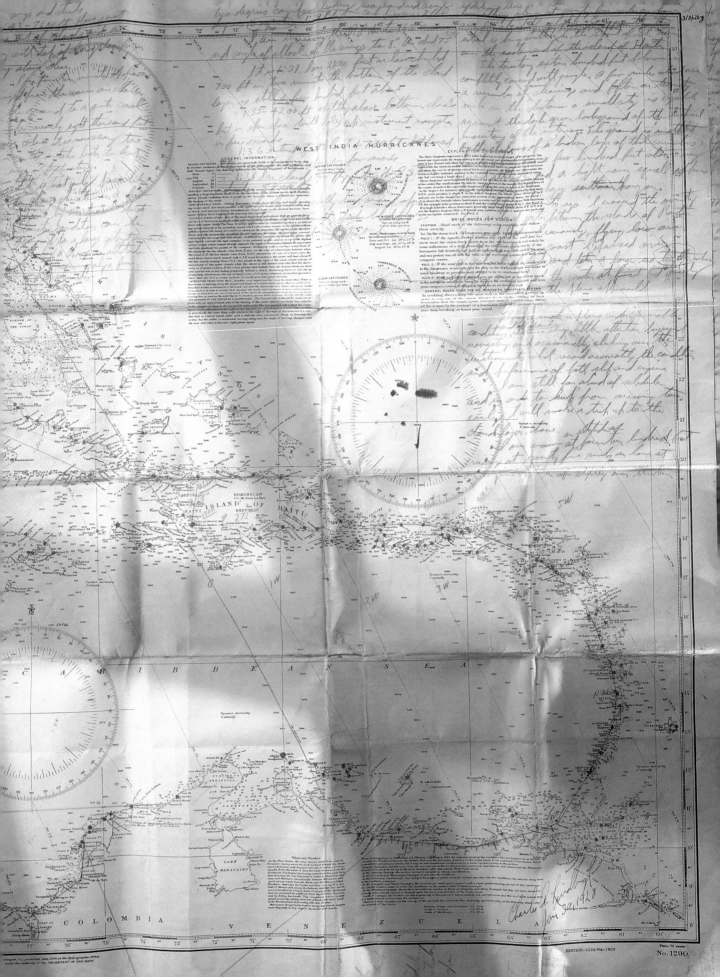

Lindbergh was well prepared for a forced landing in the rain forest. He also had two flare chutes installed before the Latin American flight so that he could make night landings. Fortunately, none of these precautions were ever needed as the *Spirit* performed impeccably as usual.

Lindbergh was wildly received by throngs in the capital cities of each of the seven Central American countries. After this, he flew on to Colombia, Venezuela, and up through the Caribbean to the Virgin Islands, Puerto Rico, the Dominican Republic, Haiti, and Cuba. At each stop a small flag of the host country was painted on each side of the *Spirit*'s aluminum cowling. So steady a pilot was Lindbergh that he actually wrote his arrival speech on the back of his aeronautical chart while in the air.

Lindbergh left Havana at the end of his tour and headed for St. Louis. This last flight of the tour should have been routine. It was not. While cruising at 4,000 feet over the Florida Straits in the morning darkness of February 13, 1928, he encountered haze and discovered that both of his new compasses had failed. Unlike the experience over the Atlantic, the magnetic compass did not swing; it spun. The needle of the earth inductor compass bounced wildly. Lindbergh was unable even to make an educated guess as to his heading.

Lost in thickening haze without a working compass, Lindbergh was in trouble. He descended in the hope of keeping in contact with the ocean and finally, with daybreak, was able to discern the faint outlines of land. But the features did not match any along the route. Eventually, he realized that the islands beneath him were not the Florida Keys but the Bahamas, some three hundred miles to the east. Lindbergh turned the *Spirit* toward Florida and soon was safely back on course, especially after his compasses began to stabilize over land. He encountered severe thunderstorms and snow as he flew north toward Lambert Field. In weather reminiscent of that which he had fought as an airmail pilot, he arrived safely in St. Louis after a fifteen-hour-and-thirty-five-minute flight.

Lindbergh decided to ground his *Spirit of St. Louis* after that flight to protect this national treasure. He had accomplished a great deal with his faithful aircraft and he felt that it was time to accede to the wishes of the nation and safely preserve the *Spirit* for the American people.

Opposite: Before arriving in Havana, Cuba, Lindbergh wrote his speech while in flight on both sides of his chart of the Caribbean. Although the aircraft was unstable, Lindbergh was able to write clearly while flying at the same time.

The Celebrity Hero

In June 1927 Lindbergh and U.S. President Calvin Coolidge (left) appear at 15 Dupont Circle, the temporary residence of the Coolidge family while repairs were being made to the White House. During the celebration held for him in Washington, Coolidge awarded Lindbergh the Distinguished Flying Cross.

I N THE UNITED STATES, popular response to Lindbergh's flight was staggering. A sampling of the celebrations held for him in Washington, D.C. and New York is indicative of the tumultuous outpouring he received. On June 12, 1927, the USS *Memphis*, with the returning hero aboard, made its way along the Virginia coast to the Chesapeake Bay "with airplanes circling overhead, destroyers guarding and convoying, sirens shrilling and multitudes cheering from the shore." In Washington, some 300,000 people turned out for a parade that began along Pennsylvania Avenue to the Washington Monument. An honor guard of cavalrymen and detachments from all branches of the armed forces rode behind Lindbergh. At the Washington Monument, President and Mrs. Coolidge greeted him. The president took the occasion to make him a colonel in the U.S. Army Air Corps Reserve and award him the Distinguished Flying Cross. Through a fifty-station radio hookup, Coolidge praised Lindbergh as "a boy representing the best tra-

Opposite: The *New York Times* carried extensive coverage of Lindbergh's achievement. It is said that the newspaper "devoted its first five pages to Lindbergh the day after his flight and the first sixteen the day after he returned from Paris."

Section 1 | "All the News That's Fit to Print." | THE WEATHER
Generally fair today and tomorrow; moderate to fresh southerly winds.
Temperature yesterday—Max., 66; Min., 54.
For weather report see Page 21.
Section 1

The New York Times.

VOL. LXXVI....No. 25,320.   · · ·   NEW YORK, SUNDAY, MAY 22, 1927.   FIVE CENTS In Manhattan (Elsewhere) and Near Borough in Emergency   TEN CENTS

LINDBERGH DOES IT! TO PARIS IN 33½ HOURS;
FLIES 1,000 MILES THROUGH SNOW AND SLEET;
CHEERING FRENCH CARRY HIM OFF FIELD

COULD HAVE GONE 500 MILES FARTHER

Gasoline for at Least That Much More Flew at Times From 10 Feet to 10,000 Feet Above Water.

ATE ONLY ONE AND A HALF OF HIS FIVE SANDWICHES

Fell Asleep at Times but Quickly Awoke—Glimpses of His Adventure in Brief Interview at the Embassy.

LINDBERGH'S OWN STORY TOMORROW.

Captain Charles A. Lindbergh was too exhausted after his arrival in Paris late last night to do more than indicate, as told below, his experiences during his flight. After he awakes today, he will narrate the full story of his remarkable exploit for readers of Monday's New York Times.

By CARLYLE MACDONALD.

Copyright, 1927, by The New York Times Company.
Special Cable to The New York Times.

PARIS, Sunday, May 22.—Captain Lindbergh was discovered at the American Embassy at 2:30 o'clock this morning. Attired in a pair of Ambassador Herrick's pajamas, he sat on the edge of a bed and talked of his flight. At the last moment Ambassador Herrick had canceled the plans of the reception committee and, by unanimous consent, took the flier to the embassy in the Place d'Iena.

A staff of American doctors who had arrived at Le Bourget Field early to minister to an "exhausted" aviator found instead a bright-eyed, smiling youth who refused to be examined.

"Oh, don't bother; I am all right," he said.

"I'd like to have a bath and a glass of milk. I would feel better," Lindbergh replied when the Ambassador asked him what he would like to have.

A bath was drawn immediately and in less than five minutes the youth had disrobed in one of the embassy guest rooms, taken his bath and was out again drinking a bottle of milk and eating a roll.

"No Use Worrying," He Tells Envoy.

"There is no use worrying about me, Mr. Ambassador," Lindbergh insisted when Mr. Herrick and members of the embassy staff wanted him to be examined by doctors and then go to bed immediately.

It was apparent that the young man was too full of his experiences to want sleep and he sat on the bed and chatted with the Ambassador, his son and daughter-in-law.

By this time a corps of frantic newspaper men who had been madly chasing the airman, following one false scent after another, had finally tracked him to the embassy. In a body they descended upon the Ambassador, who received them in the salon and informed them that he had just left Lindbergh with strict instructions to go to sleep.

As Mr. Herrick was talking with the reporters his son-in-law came downstairs and said that Lindbergh had rung and announced that he did not care to go to sleep just yet and that he would be glad to see the newspaper men for a few minutes. A cheer went up from the group who dashed by Mr. Herrick and rushed upstairs.

Expected Trouble Over Newfoundland.

In the blue and gold room, with a soft light glowing, sat the conqueror of the Atlantic. He immediately stood up and held out his hands to greet his callers. THE NEW YORK TIMES correspondent being first to greet him.

"Sit down, please," urged every one with one voice, but Lindbergh only smiled again his famous boyish smile and said:

"It's almost as easy to stand up as it is to sit down."

Questions were fired at him from all sides about his trip across the ocean, but Lindbergh seemed to dismiss them all with brief, nonchalant answers.

"I expected trouble over Newfoundland because I had been warned that the situation there was unfavorable. But I got over that hazard with no trouble whatsoever.

Sleet and Snow for 1,000 Miles.

"However, it wasn't easy going. I had sleet and snow for over 1,000 miles. Sometimes it was too high to fly over and sometimes too low to fly under, so I just had to go through it as best I could.

"I flew as low as 10 feet in some places and as high as 10,000 in others. I passed no ships in the daytime, but at night I saw the lights of several ships, the night being bright and clear."

Everyone then wanted to know if the flier had been sleepy on the voyage.

"I didn't really get what you might call downright sleepy," he said, "but I think I sort of nodded several times. In fact, I could have flown half that distance again. I had enough fuel

Continued on Page Five.

LEVINE ABANDONS BELLANCA FLIGHT

Venture Given Up as Designer Splits With Him—Plane Narrowly Escapes Burning.

BYRD'S CRAFT IS NAMED

Lindbergh Cheered at Ceremony—Commander, Now Last in Field, Waits on Weather.

Through no fault of his own, Clarence D. Chamberlin, who with Bert Acosta established a world's non-stop flying record a few weeks ago, will not fly the record-breaking monoplane in an attempt to establish a second New York-Paris non-stop flight.

C. M. Bellanca, designer of the plane, and Charles S. Levine of the Columbia Aircraft Company, owner of the ship, came to the parting of the ways last night and the designer finally severed his connection with the promoter. Then Levine issued a statement that the proposed flight, which has been talked of for weeks, was off.

The statement said:

"Due to the crowning blow of Mr. Bellanca's resignation, the plane will be placed in the hangar. Mr. Bellanca's resignation causes us to abandon plans for the New York-Paris flight for the present."

At the very moment that the statement was issued the plane was near the runway at Roosevelt Field with gas tanks filled and oil and equipment aboard ready for the start for Paris.

Plane Threatened by Fire.

A few minutes later, as it was being wheeled off, preparatory to being housed for the night, it narrowly escaped being destroyed by fire. When the word came to the field that the flight was definitely off, mechanics were ordered to empty one gasoline tank to lighten the machine. The gasoline spilled on the ground and while the ship was being towed away a careless spectator threw the stub of a lighted cigarette down.

In an instant there was a terrific flare and a dense burst of smoke as the gasoline blazed up.

"The Bellanca's gone," was the cry that rose from thousands of spectators who had gathered at the field.

Word was flashed to the army air station at Mitchel Field that there had been an accident and ambulances and fire-fighting apparatus were sent across the road. An ambulance from the Nassau County Hospital at Mineola was also sent to Roosevelt Field, as well as fire apparatus from Mineola.

The plane, however, was "beyond the danger line and was not injured.

It had been announced that the Columbia would take off at 8 o'clock and Chamberlin was in his flying clothes ready to climb into the cockpit with the unnamed pilot who was to have accompanied him on the trip.

With the elimination of the Bellanca monoplane, only Lieut.

Continued on Page Four.

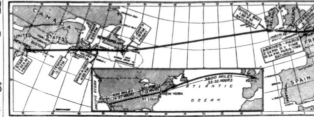

CAPTAIN CHARLES A. LINDBERGH,
Who Flew Alone Across the Atlantic, New York to Paris, in Thirty-three and One-half Hours.

Times Wide World Photo.

New York Stages Big Celebration After Hours of Anxious Waiting

Harbor Craft, Factories, Fire Sirens and Radio Carry Message of the Flier's Victory Throughout the City—Theatres Halt While Audiences Cheer.

New York bubbled all day yesterday with excitement and expectancy, first yearning for word of Captain Lindbergh, then half-doubting, gaining confidence as the afternoon progressed and finally acclaiming the victory of the young aviator with street / demonstrations where the crowds were thickest, in which the ancient phrase, "I told you so," was often repeated. It was evident during the day that New York had confidence in the lad from the West.

On the streets and elsewhere Lindbergh was the one topic of conversation the whole day long. In the subway, on the elevated, in trains and cars, motion picture houses, theatres, wherever a few had gathered, or even where one man could find another to talk to, one heard "Lindbergh — Lindbergh — Lindbergh."

And such expressions as this:

"He'll make it, all right."

"Some baby!"

"Well, if he's hit Ireland, he's safe anyway."

"He's away ahead of his time."

"What's the difference in time between here and there, anyway?"

Confused On Difference in Time.

To this latter question there were some amusing answers. One woman who had the aviator's running time mixed with the difference in time between New York and Paris solemnly informed her companion that there was thirty-six hours difference.

She said it with an air which signified: "I don't mean maybe." A surprising number of persons insisted that the difference in time was three hours.

Early in the day, even before there was any good reason why there should be definite news, the interest of the people was demonstrated in two ways. At every news stand there were little groups scanning the headlines and buying newspapers. In every newspaper office the switchboards were literally swamped with inquiries. It was not sufficient that the operator said there was no word, or, later, that Lindbergh's plane had been seen over Ireland. The inquirers wanted specific information:

"Well, when will you get the first news?" they asked. And later:

"If he's over Ireland how long will it be before he gets to Paris?"

"Is he all right?"

The questions that were asked, considering that no news could possibly come direct from Captain Lindbergh before he landed, are as surprising as the guesses at the difference in time.

The Times Gets 10,000 Phone Calls.

The telephone inquiries came from all sorts of people and all directions. Not a few rang up THE TIMES office and apologetically explained that they were on golf links or elsewhere at a distance, and hence could not

Continued on Page Six.

LINDBERGH TRIUMPH THRILLS COOLIDGE

President Cables Praise to "Heroic Flier" and Concern for Nungesser and Coli.

CAPITAL THROBS WITH JOY

Kellogg, New, MacNider, Patrick and Many More Join in Paying Tribute to Daring Youth.

Special to The New York Times.

WASHINGTON, May 21.—The triumph of Captain Charles A. Lindbergh in flying from New York to Paris without a stop created a tremendous sensation in the national capital and found immediate response in a host of official messages and statements congratulating the daring aviator upon his achievement.

President Coolidge expressed his admiration in a message transmitted through Ambassador Herrick in Paris for delivery to the young flier in person.

With a single possible exception, this city has never been more thrilled since the armistice, when Woodrow Wilson mingled with many thousands in celebrating the end of the war. The exception was when Walter Johnson arose from apparent defeat and won the deciding world series baseball game in 1924.

"The American people," the President said, "rejoice with me at the brilliant termination of your heroic flight. The first non-stop flight of a lone aviator across the Atlantic crowns the record of American aviation, and in bringing the greetings of the American people to France you likewise carry the assurance of our admiration of those intrepid Frenchmen, Nungesser and Coli, whose bold spirits first ventured on your exploit, and likewise a message of our continued anxiety concerning their fate."

Secretary Kellogg, in a message similarly transmitted, said:

"I heartily congratulate you on the success of your great adventure in accomplishing a non-stop flight from New York to Paris. It is a great step in the advancement of aviation. Every one in the United States is proud of your accomplishment."

Knew Lindbergh as a Boy.

In a statement issued here Mr. Kellogg referred to his personal friendship for Lindbergh, whom he has known for years through the young man's late father, a Representative in Congress from the Secretary's home State of Minnesota.

"News has just reached me," Mr. Kellogg said, "of the success of Lindbergh in completing his flight from New York to Paris. It is an achievement of which every American can justly be proud. I have known Lindbergh since he was a boy and rejoice at this culmination of his ambitions, which could only have been gained by scientific knowledge, superb courage and physique and sterling character. Our rejoicing in Lindbergh's success, however, is tempered by our continued ignorance of the fate of Nungesser and Coli, whose courage and valor have now been equaled, but cannot be surpassed."

Hanford MacNider, Acting Secre-

Continued on Page Six.

CROWD ROARS THUNDEROUS WELCOME

Breaks Through Lines of Soldiers and Police and Surging to Plane Lifts Weary Flier from His Cockpit

AVIATORS RESCUE HIM FROM FRENZIED MOB OF 25,000

Paris Boulevards Ring With Celebration After Day and Night Watch—American Flag Is Called For and Wildly Acclaimed.

By EDWIN L. JAMES.

Copyright, 1927, by The New York Times Company.
Special Cable to The New York Times.

PARIS, May 21.—Lindbergh did it. Twenty minutes after 10 o'clock tonight suddenly and softly there slipped out of the darkness a gray-white airplane as 25,000 pairs of eyes strained toward it. At 10:24 the Spirit of St. Louis landed and lines of soldiers, ranks of policemen and stout steel fences went down before a mad rush as irresistible as the tides of the ocean.

"Well, I made it," smiled Lindbergh, as the little white monoplane came to a halt in the middle of the field and the first vanguard reached the plane. Lindbergh made a move to jump out. Twenty hands reached for him and lifted him out as if he were a baby. Several thousands in a minute were around the plane. Thousands more broke the barriers of iron rails round the field, cheering wildly.

Lifted From His Cockpit.

As he was lifted to the ground Lindbergh was pale, and, with his hair unkempt, he looked completely worn out. He had strength enough, however, to smile, and waved his hand to the crowd. Soldiers with fixed bayonets were unable to keep back the crowd.

United States Ambassador Herrick was among the first to welcome and congratulate the hero.

A NEW YORK TIMES man was one of the first to reach the machine after its graceful descent to the field. Those first to arrive at the plane had a picture that will live in their minds for the rest of their lives. His cap off, his famous locks falling in disarray around his eyes, "Lucky Lindy" sat peering out over over the rim of the little cockpit of his machine.

Dramatic Scene at the Field.

It was high drama. Picture the scene. Twenty to twenty-five thousand people were massed on the east side of Le Bourget air field. Some of them had been there six and seven hours.

Off to the left the giant phare lighthouse of Mount Valerien flashed its guiding light 300 miles into the air. Closer on the left Le Bourget Lighthouse twinkled, and off to the right another giant revolving phare sent its beams high into the heavens.

Big arc lights on all sides with enormous electric glares were flooding the landing field. From time to time rockets rose and burst in varied lights over the field.

Seven thirty, the hour announced for the arrival, had come and gone. Then 8 o'clock came, and no Lindbergh; at 9 o'clock the sun had set but then came reports that Lindbergh had been seen over Cork. Then he had been seen over Valentia in Ireland and then over Plymouth.

Suddenly a message spread like lightning, the aviator had been seen over Cherbourg. However, remembering the messages telling of Captain Nungesser's flight, the crowd was skeptical.

"One chance in a thousand!" "Oh, he cannot do it without navigating instruments!" "It's a pity, because he was a brave boy." Pessimism had spread over the great throng by 10 o'clock.

The stars came out and a chill wind blew.

Watchers Are Twice Disappointed.

Suddenly the field lights flooded their glares onto the landing ground and there came the roar of an airplane's motor. The crowd was still, then began a cheer, but two minutes later the landing glares went dark for the searchlight had identified the plane and it was not Captain Lindbergh's.

Stamping their feet in the cold, the crowd waited patiently. It seemed quite apparent that nearly every one was willing to wait all night, hoping against hope.

Suddenly—it was 10:16 exactly—another motor roared over the heads of the crowd. In the sky one caught a glimpse of a white gray plane, and for an instant heard the sound of one. Then it dimmed, and the idea spread that it was yet another disappointment.

Again landing lights glared and almost by the time they had flooded the field the gray-white plane had lighted on the far side nearly half a mile from the crowd. It seemed to stop almost as it hit the ground, so gently did it land.

And then occurred a scene which almost passed description. Two companies of soldiers with fixed bayonets and the Le Bourget field police, reinforced by Paris agents, had held the crowd in good order. But as the lights showed the plane

Lindbergh's mother, Evangeline Lodge Land Lindbergh, is pictured visiting the pilot in New York.

ditions of this country . . . this wholesome, earnest, fearless, courageous product of America . . . a valiant character, driven by an unconquerable will and inspired by the imagination and the spirit of his Viking ancestors . . . set wing across the dangerous stretches of the North Atlantic. . . .The absence of self-acclaim, the refusal to become commercialized, which has marked the conduct of this sincere and genuine exemplar of fine and noble virtues, has endeared him to everyone. He has returned unspoiled." After the ceremonies, Lindbergh was informed by Dr. Charles G. Abbot, acting secretary, that the Smithsonian Institution had nominated him for the Langley Medal, the highest honor given by the institution.[13]

The next day, after flying from Washington to Mitchel Field, Long Island, Lindbergh was flown to New York Bay, where he was greeted by Grover A. Whalen, Chairman of the Mayor's Reception Committee. The municipal reception boat *Macom*, accompanied by a marine honor guard made up of some four hundred ships, ferried him to the Battery. The overblown description of the scene provided by the *New York Times'* publication, *Current History,* is instructive: "Never before was there such a harbor demonstration. Stodgy tugs decked in flags pranced on the waves and bumped against each other like bear cubs at play. Sedate ferries clad in flying bunting nosed motor boats from their prows. Fireboats shot streams of water at the sun. River steamers staggered under the weight of passengers massed on one side. Smoke and steam from wide-open whistles clouded the sky." Once on land, Lindbergh was greeted by his mother and then was driven up Broadway to City Hall amidst "a paper snowstorm [that] enveloped the canyons of lower New York in a mist of white" while "the air was split with the shrill uproar of tens of thousands of sirens, tooters and full-throated whistles and the huzzas of hundreds of thousands of welcoming citizens." An estimated four million people thronged to the city's celebratory ticker tape parade, orchestrated by Mayor Jimmy Walker, an event, it was said, that "surpassed any reception ever accorded a private citizen in American history."[14]

At City Hall, Mayor Walker gave Lindbergh an illuminated scroll of honor and pinned the Medal of Valor on him, a gift of the City and the American Scenic and Historic Preservation Society. Lindbergh and the mayor then proceeded up Fifth Avenue to Central Park. There, Governor Alfred E. Smith presented Lindbergh with a medal from New York State, awarded for "courage and intrepidity of the highest degree in flying alone and unaided from New York to Paris, to the glory of his country and his own undying fame." A few days later, Lindbergh was feted at a banquet at the Commodore Hotel. Typical of the gush was an address by former Secretary of State Charles Evans Hughes in which he said, "This is the happiest day, the happiest day of all days for America, which as one mind is now intent upon the noblest and the best. America as picturing to herself youth with the highest aims, with courage unsurpassed; science victorious. Last and not least, motherhood, with her loveliest crown."[15]

In addition to the official celebrations, there was the reaction by the press. Historian Daniel Boorstin estimates that "to tell about this young man on the day after his flight, the nation's newspapers used 25,000 tons of newsprint more than usual. In many places sales were two to five times normal, and might have been higher if the presses could have turned out more newspapers." In *The Right Stuff*, Tom Wolfe says that the *New York Times* "devoted its first five pages to Lindbergh the day after his flight and the first *sixteen* the day after he returned from Paris, and all other major newspapers tried to keep up."[16]

Bulk, however, was not the only measure of Lindbergh's esteem in the press. A sampling of the newspaper and magazine coverage of the event suggests that the press looked upon Lindbergh's accomplishment in Promethean terms and strained for the language to describe deeds of great courage. On May 23, the *New York Times* ran an editorial titled "The Saga of Lindbergh" that suggested Lindbergh's similarity to the Norsemen: "There is a poetic fitness in the fact that an American of Scandinavian descent should have been the first to make the successful venture into the air over a course with a thousand miles of sleet and snow such as the vikings faced in their early voyages. . . . As such the saga of CHARLES LINDBERGH will be sung through years to come. It will be repeated by youth, and especially American youth, for more years than the traditional story of the Marathon runner or the mythical Icarus who flew too near the sun."[17]

Laurence Goldstein places all of this hyperbole in proper perspective. He claims that Lindbergh's transatlantic flight "remains so clouded by the aura of ballyhoo that even at this distance it seems to belong less to the history of aviation than to the triumph of that inflated rhetoric we have come to recognize and distrust as media hype. . . . The official account of the flight prepared for the Boy Scouts of America called it 'all things considered, the greatest feat undertaken by a single man.'" Goldstein concludes that "a historian must back away from such eulogies, but not so far that he loses sight of their contribution to the essential character of the event. Lindbergh himself recognized that the authors of such words did not praise him so much as their own Platonic conception of greatness, which they thrust upon him. Those who worked themselves into a rhetorical frenzy of celebration were not, he felt, responding to his achievement, about which he had no false modesty, but to the hangover of journalistic practice in nineteenth-century America."[18]

Daniel Boorstin's assessment is similar. He says that Lindbergh "performed singledhanded one of the heroic deeds of the century" and that "his deed was heroic in the best epic mold." Nevertheless, Boorstin says, "the biggest news about Lindbergh was that he was such big news . . . Lindbergh's well-knownness was so sudden and so overwhelming. It was easy to make stories about what a big celebrity he was . . . there was little else anyone could say about him. Lindbergh's singularly impressive heroic deed was soon far overshadowed by his even more impressive publicity. If well-knownness made a celebrity, here was the greatest. Of course it was remarkable to fly the ocean by oneself, but far more remarkable thus to dominate the news. His stature as hero was nothing compared with his stature as celebrity. All the more because it had happened, literally, overnight."[19]

New York City honored Lindbergh with a ticker tape parade that was attended by an estimated crowd of four million. One publication wrote that the event "surpassed any reception ever accorded a private citizen in American history."

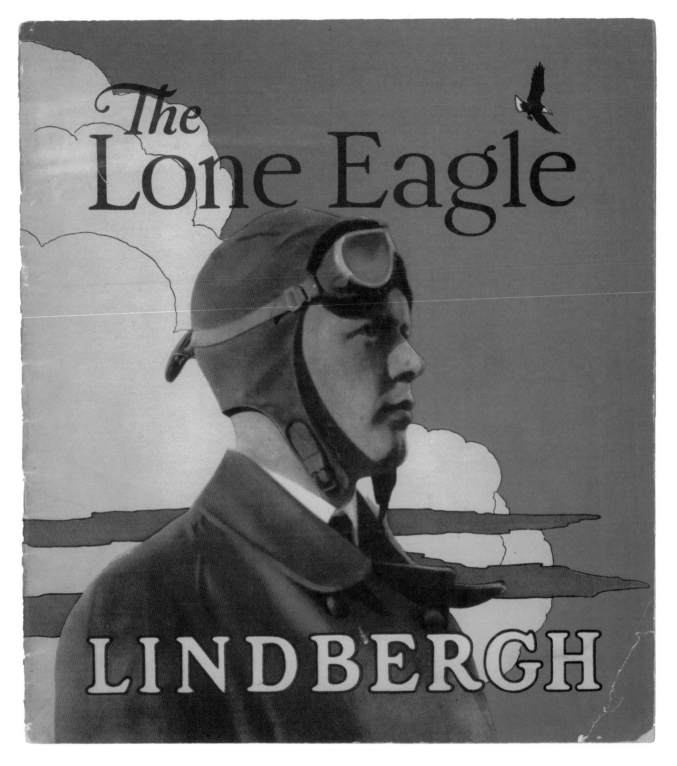

The Lone Eagle

LINDBERGH

This celebratory print is an example of the memorabilia created to commemorate Lindbergh's transatlantic flight.

Opposite: A children's book about Lindbergh was published in 1929 to take advantage of the overwhelming public interest in his flight.

This sheet music devoted to Lindbergh is part of the Bella C. Landauer Collection in the library of the
National Air and Space Museum, Smithsonian Institution, Washington, D.C. The musical compositions range
in style from marches to fox trots to waltzes.

Opposite, above: These commemorative pins and medallions honoring Lindbergh are from the
collection of the National Air and Space Museum, Smithsonian Institution, Washington, D.C.

Opposite, below: "Lindy—The New Flying Game," developed by Parker Brothers, is typical
of the genre of popular culture items devoted to Lindbergh resulting from his celebrity.

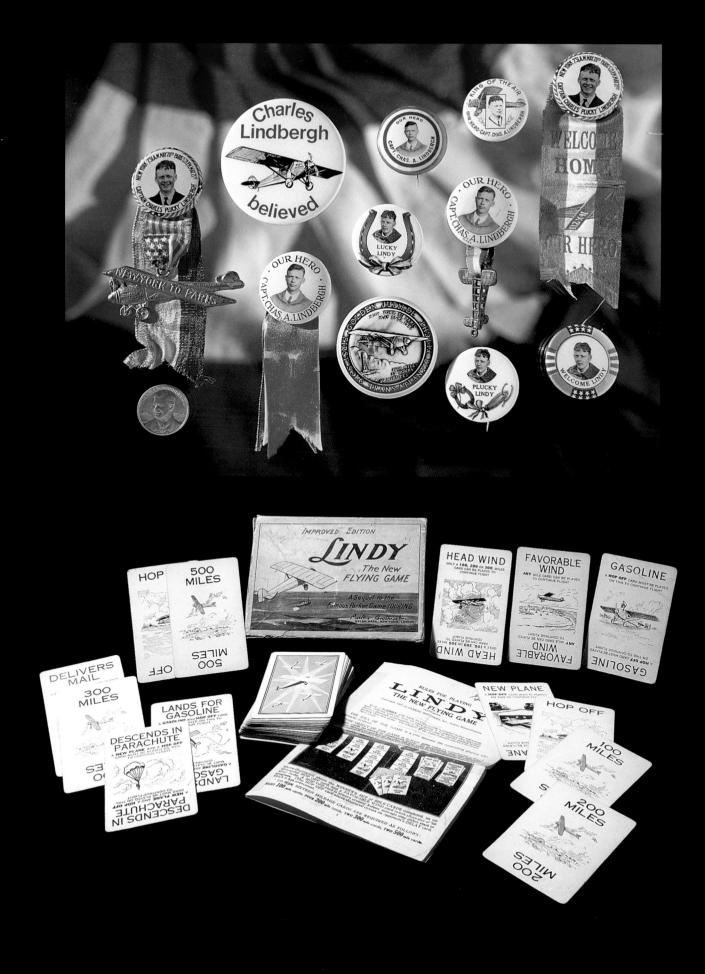

HOW DOES ONE BEGIN TO ACCOUNT FOR THE LINDBERGH PHENOMENON? Certainly, the fact that he dared to test himself alone against the formidable ocean made him a hero in the eyes of many. The Atlantic was four times wider at its narrowest point than the longest distance that had ever been flown over water at the end of World War I. It was also treacherous. Weather over the Atlantic could blow an aircraft miles off course in a few moment's time or coat it in an impenetrable layer of ice and send it plummeting into a watery abyss. The route considered best for flying the Atlantic was far to the north of the customary shipping lanes, making rescue from a crash very unlikely.

A more emblematic explanation for the Lindbergh phenomenon is that to a nation transformed by World War I and the turbulent era of the 1920s, Lindbergh and his flight represented a way to reconcile traditional American values with the increasingly complex and confusing new technological age. In his essay on Lindbergh's flight, John William Ward remarks that Lindbergh's achievement enabled the American public to look simultaneously backward to the frontier and forward to the technological future and to celebrate the machine that enabled him to accomplish his feat.[20]

Yet another, more elemental aspect of the American response to Lindbergh accommodates the public's perception of aviation as merely stunt flying, an activity for idiots, or for those with a recklessly self-destructive urge. In fact, many people, influenced by the press, looked upon Lindbergh's flight as senseless, and this is evidenced by the epithets "Lucky Lindy" and "The Flying Fool." This is hardly surprising. By the 1920s, the stereotype of the brash, risk-taking aviator was firmly fixed in the public mind. Sensational reporting of aircraft accidents, devil-may-care barnstormers, and daring tales of aerial combat in World War I conditioned public attitudes about pilots and flying before and after Lindbergh. These influences were perhaps more important than the notions of pioneering or technological progress. The vast public, largely unaware of the careful planning that was designed to minimize Lindbergh's risk, simply saw him as a fantastically reckless adventurer, a kind of holy fool.

Then there is the question of the significance of the transatlantic flight itself. Does the period of the airplane's influence on American society, as has often been noted, have as its point of demarcation the moment that Lindbergh set the wheels of the *Spirit of St. Louis* down on the runway at Le Bourget? The flight may have been a catalyst for aviation in the United States, but as some commentators have pointed out, the seeds of a viable national aviation effort had been planted long before Lindbergh's appearance in the forefront of the news in 1927, and Americans had been conscious of aviation from the time of World War I.

Throughout the twenties, as aviation slowly began to become a practical means of transportation, aviation technology grew to meet the demands of practicality. One manifestation of the utility of aircraft was the U.S. Air Mail Service, inaugurated on May 15, 1918, with flights from Washington to New York, with Philadelphia as an intermediate stop. Although the earliest scheduled airmail flights were made by U.S. Army pilots, the Post Office Department took over the service in August 1918. The airmail was responsible for a number of aviation technology milestones. The most important of these—the development of lighted airways—was achieved on August 31, 1923, when forty-two landing fields on the Chicago to Cheyenne airmail route were illuminated by rotating electric arc beacons whose light was visible for fifty miles. A shortage of funds caused the system to close down shortly after its inauguration, but the following summer the first regular night airmail service was instituted. Mail flying could now take place on a day-and-night basis, and the time it took to fly across the continent was reduced to approximately thirty-two hours as compared to the seventy-eight-and-a-half-hour combination air-rail service originated in September 1920.

Other practical milestones in aviation during the 1920s were forthcoming. The passage of the Contract Air Mail Act on February 2, 1925 (the so-called Kelly Act, after its sponsor), enabled the Post Office Department to turn over carriage of the airmail to private contractors. The act's effect on aviation was such that it laid the groundwork for a strong air transportation industry by allowing the private carriers to make a sufficient profit from airmail transport so that they could finance the carriage of passengers and cargo. R. E. G. Davies had commented that the act was "the first major legislative step towards the creation of an airline industry in the United States." In addition, the Air Commerce Act (Bingham-Merritt-Parker Bill) of 1926 fostered the development of commercial aviation in the United States by giving the Department of Commerce complete jurisdiction over aircraft and pilot licensing and the building and maintenance of airways and navigational facilities, as well as responsibility for air safety, which by 1926 had become a major issue.[21]

The period from 1916 to 1926 was also noteworthy in that four events occurred that began what might be termed "the incorporation of aviation;" in other words, its transformation from sport-recreation activity to business enterprise. First, by settling the patent dispute that the Wright brothers had created late in 1909 with their suit against Glenn Curtiss and, subsequently, others, and creating a cross-licensing agreement and the Manufacturers Aircraft Association, the industry overcame a barrier to technological innovation and had begun to legitimize aviation as a business. Second, during World War I, the alliance that executives in the automotive industry forged with the fledgling aviation industry was a significant step in standardizing aviation business practice. Third, Clement Keys's takeover of the Curtiss Aeroplane and Motor Corporation, the first successful aeronautical corporation, and the anticipated merger of the Curtiss and Wright interests—two of the most successful aviation enterprises of the period—indicate that the industry was beginning to be tied to Wall Street and the world of finance. Fourth, through the industry's association with the automobile industry and the efforts of the Guggenheim Fund for the Promotion of Aeronautics, aeronautical engineering was becoming a recognized profession, further legitimizing aviation as a commercial venture.

Notwithstanding the importance of these accomplishments to the development of aeronautics in the United States, public perception of aviation during the 1920s was conditioned, as has been suggested, not so much by executive boards and legislative hearings or by technological progress in aviation as by sensational aircraft accidents, devil-may-care barnstorming aviators, and popular films about aviation, among other factors. In this scenario of the Lindbergh mythos, the two seemingly contradictory ideas—John William Ward's pioneer-technologist and the public's brash, risk-taking pilot—merge into a resolution. As Michael Sherry has pointed out, "the disasters were as essential a part of aviation's image as the records set and inventions tested. . . . Few wanted to hear Lindbergh say that his famous flight involved slight risk." Indeed, if one calculates the close calls Lindbergh had in the barnstorming and parachuting days that led up to the transatlantic flight, and the careful preparation for the flight, one cannot fail to be impressed how closely tied risk-taking and technological advancement in aviation were during the period.[22]

In the final analysis, it is probably fair to say that Lindbergh's transatlantic flight was important in that it made the public aware of aviation in a way that it had not been aware of it before. As Kenneth Davis points out, "future historians might have difficulty determining how much of the great aviation boom was due to Lindbergh and how much to other factors. . . . But none could doubt that he was a major cause of it." After Lindbergh's famous flight, and this is where his importance has been neglected, popular enthusiasm for flying took on new dimensions. Technological and commercial progress continued to be made, with Lindbergh at the forefront of the movement to make aviation a viable commercial venture. More

Anne Morrow Lindbergh is seated in the Lockheed Sirius *Tingmissartoq* in 1933 at Karlskrona, Sweden, Lindbergh's ancestral home. This flight, on which Anne served as copilot and navigator, was undertaken in an attempt to survey transatlantic air routes between North America and Europe.

important, however, the flight captured the popular imagination and became manifest in the culture of the period. Pulp fiction, advertising, films, the comics, industrial and automotive design, and vernacular architecture were just a few of the areas that borrowed heavily from aviation in the 1930s. Moreover, Lindbergh's flight reinforced the image of the airplane as a machine of progress, savior of American ideals, and symbol of a future transformed by technology. The airplane could lead the United States into a technical Utopia, while reclaiming the values of the past. In large part thanks to Lindbergh, the airplane became one of the most conspicuous symbols of the Depression era.[23]

DESPITE THE ADULATION OF THE PRESS AND PUBLIC, Lindbergh soon began to tire of what he thought was the undue attention paid to him and the invasion of his privacy, and he began to react against the press and the public. The first signs of a rupture appeared even before the transatlantic flight. Lindbergh was especially annoyed with the press for the way they treated his mother, particularly the way they upset her with questions about the danger involved in making such a hazardous flight. Lindbergh insisted that reporters had no right to pry into his personal life, and would only answer questions about aviation and the transatlantic flight. Unlike other notable figures, he refused to give reporters what they wanted; namely, tidbits about his exploits in the air and details of his personal life. The situation with the press worsened considerably in the aftermath of Lindbergh's transatlantic flight and his marriage to Anne Morrow.

Incidents with the press and public multiplied. A typical one occurred in April 1928, after Lindbergh had returned from his good-will tour of Latin America and was on his way to New York to meet the body of the recently deceased Myron T. Herrick. Lindbergh landed at Bolling Field in Washington, D.C. for a meeting with Major Thomas G. Lanphier of the U.S. Army Air Corps. According to an account in the *New York Times,* "a small crowd had been waiting for several hours on the water-soaked field. . . . The crowd rushed toward the plane and when the leaders had nearly reached it, Colonel Lindbergh suddenly raced the motor and swung the plane around and out into the field, the strong slip stream from the motor throwing up mud and water. . . . Major Lanphier drove out to the plane and clambered upon a wing. When the photographers and some of the more courageous of the crowd drew near again, Colonel Lindbergh raced the motor, for a second time, driving the plane across the field and spattering the crowd once more. The photographers, deserted by the crowd, made one more attempt and suffered a third time." Although widely reported, the incident was not given much attention. In August 1929, at the National Air Races in Cleveland, Lindbergh's aircraft caught in his slipstream an approaching commercial airliner carrying thirteen passengers. The airliner "rocked furiously," but the captain managed to bring it safely to the ground. The incident went uninvestigated.[24]

Despite Lindbergh's value as a celebrity, the press became unhappy over what it perceived as his ungrateful attitude toward them; after all, they believed that they had "created him." Lindbergh, on the other hand, continued to insist that any subject other than his desire to promote aviation was out of bounds for reporters. The tension grew until it could not be contained. According to Kenneth Davis, "abruptly, there developed an estrangement between hero and working press which grew rapidly into a cold war, all the more bitter because reporters could not publish their grievances." Davis contends that "it was not Lindbergh's refusal to become their puppet which outraged newsmen. Rather it was a growing suspicion that they had become *his* puppets. It had become an article of bitter faith among newsmen that Lindbergh was pulling strings they themselves had fashioned (the irony was maddening), making them dance to his private tunes while treating them personally with a cold arrogant contempt. Some of them even came to believe that the strings he used had actually been designed by him—for the superstition was soon widely prevalent among journalists that no element of the 'glory' of this 'shy, modest youth' was or ever had been inadvertent on his part. From their point of view, he really had discovered the secret of using fame, compounded of other people's emotions, as a kind of energy; he now harnessed it, they believed, not primarily in service of the 'cause' to which he was so ostentatiously dedicated, but for the satisfaction of his own enormous appetite for Power." In contrast to the press, the public's attitude toward Lindbergh remained worshipful.[25]

Lindbergh's patience with the press and public reached breaking point when his son, Charles, Jr., was kidnapped from the family home in Hopewell, New Jersey, in March 1932. Like the transatlantic flight, the kidnapping elicited an exaggerated reaction from the press. Reporters swarmed en masse onto the Lindbergh estate looking for stories and interviews, not only making themselves unpleasant but jeopardizing both the investigation and the return of the baby. After the dead baby's body was discovered in May 1932, there were reports that press photographers had

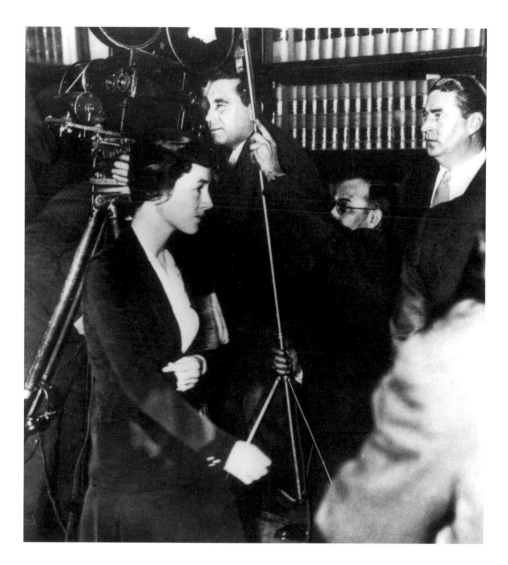

Bruno Richard Hauptmann was convicted in February 1935 and executed in April 1936 for the kidnapping and murder of the Lindberghs' first-born son Charles, Jr. Anne Morrow Lindbergh attended the trial amidst the media circus that surrounded the family at the time.

The Fairchild FC-2, that Lindbergh stands before was flown by Philip R. Love, Lindbergh's fellow pilot in the Army Air Service and at Robertson Aircraft Corporation, during the 1927 Guggenheim Fund aerial tour of the United States.

tried to photograph it in a Trenton mortuary. Although the furor died down after the baby's corpse was found, the arrest of a suspect, Bruno Richard Hauptmann, in September 1934, and his trial in January and February 1935, reignited the issue and gave rise to more lurid coverage by the press, which dragged on for weeks and months. To make matters worse, after Hauptmann's conviction, the Lindberghs received an increasing number of death threats against their son Jon, who had been born shortly after the Lindbergh baby, Charles, had been found dead.

In December 1935, largely as a result of the kidnapping and its aftermath, Lindbergh and his wife and son fled the United States for England. From Harold Nicolson, British diplomat, writer, and biographer of Dwight Morrow, they leased Long Barn, a cottage belonging to Nicolson in Kent. (In the summer of 1938, the Lindberghs moved to Illiec, an island off the coast of Brittany, where they were neighbors with Dr. Alexis Carrel, Lindbergh's friend and collaborator on the development of a heart perfusion pump.) Not long after leaving the United States, the Lindberghs visited Nazi Germany, spending several weeks there hosted by Nazi aviation leaders Hermann Goering (head of the Luftwaffe, the German air force) and Ernst Udet, the World War I flying ace. Lindbergh even accepted a German Aero Club emblem presented by Erhard Milch, the Luftwaffe's production chief. These visits, and Lindbergh's assessment of German air power, would cause a great deal of controversy.[26]

In 1936, Major Truman Smith, military attaché to the American embassy in Berlin, whose responsibility it was to gather intelligence on the German military, realized that the Luftwaffe was becoming a major weapon in Germany's arsenal. Not having much knowledge of aviation himself, Smith realized that he needed an expert to assess the German air situation. Smith's wife called his attention to an article in the *Paris Herald* on Lindbergh's recent visit to an aircraft factory in France,

Lindbergh appears with Major Truman Smith, military attaché to the American Embassy in Berlin (right), during one of his numerous trips to Germany in the mid-to-late 1930s. Lindbergh was convinced that the German air force was superior to any in the world.

and Smith immediately thought of asking Lindbergh to assist him. Lindbergh accepted Smith's invitation to tour specific facilities in Germany—military units, bases, factories—writing to his mother that he was "looking forward, with great interest, to going there. Even under the difficulties she has encountered since the war, Germany has taken part in a number of aviation developments. . . ."[27]

In July 1936, Lindbergh and his wife arrived in Berlin. While in Germany, Lindbergh, among other things, visited the Junkers plant at Dessau, spent a day with a crack Luftwaffe fighter squadron, the Richthofen Geschwader, and spent a day at the air research institute at Adlershof. On the basis of what he had seen, Lindbergh concluded that Germany was "now able to produce military aircraft faster than any European country. Possibly even faster than we could in the States for the first few weeks after we started competitions." Moreover, he believed that there was "a spirit in Germany which I have not seen in any other country. There is certainly great ability, and I am inclined to think more intelligent leadership than is generally recognized. A person would have to be blind not to realize that they have already built up tremendous strength."[28]

During his week in Germany, Lindbergh, accompanied by his wife, took part in three significant social events in his honor: an Aero Club luncheon; a formal luncheon hosted by Hermann Goering at his official residence on the Wilhelm Strasse; and attendance at the 1936 Olympics in Berlin. Despite expressing some fears about the militarization of Germany and the potential of air power as a quick and destructive weapon, Lindbergh wrote that Germany was "the most interesting nation in the world today, and that she is attempting to find a solution for some of our most fundamental problems." To some American Jews, Lindbergh's visit to Germany had overtones of impropriety. Lindbergh had been cautioned by Harry Guggenheim's brother-in-law, Roger Straus, not to allow his visit to be used by the German propaganda machine as an interpretation of his approval of the regime, and Harry himself wrote to Lindbergh that he had "every confidence that you would conduct yourself as to give no air to anti-Semitism." Nevertheless, the Lindberghs' enthusiasm for the Third Reich would stir up a great deal of controversy. Especially galling to Americans, as Walter L. Hixson points out, was that "the image of Lindbergh, grim-faced as he departed his native country, now reappeared in press photographs that showed him flashing his broad smile in the company of Nazi leaders."[29]

In the fall of 1937, Lindbergh and Anne returned to Germany. On this trip Lindbergh visited airfields and factories, including the Focke-Wulf plant in Bremen, where he saw a demonstration of an aircraft that could fly vertically. After the tour, Lindbergh helped Major Smith prepare Report #15540, "General Estimate [of Germany's Air Power] of November 1, 1937." The report concluded that "a highly competent observer" [Lindbergh] estimated that "if the present progress curves [of America and Germany] should continue as they have in the past two years, Germany should obtain technical parity with the USA by 1941 or 1942." In his memoirs, published years later, Smith stated that because of his unfamiliarity with air matters, the conclusions of the report were for the most part Lindbergh's— "many of the paragraphs are couched in Lindbergh's exact words." Smith makes clear that the report "sought to convey to those leaders of the American armed forces, who were not themselves aviators, the strength level German air power had attained by November 1, 1937." Smith states that the assessment of German air power was "dependent on four factors: (1) the efficiency of its aeronautical science, (2) the capacity of its aircraft and aircraft motor industry, (3) the performance of its combat planes, and (4) the training level attained by its personnel. The report also sought to compare the overall combat value of the Luftwaffe with that of the Royal Air Force and the French Air Arm."[30]

On Lindbergh's third trip to Germany in October 1938, he accepted the Service Cross of the German Eagle (with Star) from Hermann Goering, which created a wave of adverse publicity. Although there was no immediate reaction to the incident, it had come shortly before *Kristallnacht,* a vicious Nazi pogrom on November 9–10 in which many synagogues were burned, houses and shops owned by Jews were destroyed, and tens of thousands of Jews were taken off to confinement camps. To make matters worse, the Lindberghs had been thinking of moving to Berlin, and this information was used against them. Among the most scathing criticism were the comments of Secretary of the Interior Harold L. Ickes,

Lindbergh and his wife visited Germany several times in the late 1930s, occasionally meeting with members of the Nazi Party.

made in a speech to a Zionist meeting in Cleveland in November 1938. Ickes criticized Lindbergh for accepting an award "at the hands of a brutal dictator who with the same hand is robbing and torturing thousands of fellow human beings" and he declared that anyone who would accept a decoration from Germany also "forfeits his right to be an American." Relatives and friends of the family urged the Lindberghs not to move to Berlin and for Lindbergh to return the medal. Although they chose to live in Paris rather than Berlin, Charles refused to give back the medal, arguing "that the returning of decorations which were given in times of peace, and as a gesture of friendship, can have no constructive effect."[31]

To add fuel to the fire, before the medal incident, Lindbergh and his wife had made a trip to the Soviet Union in August 1938 to inspect air facilities. The couple had been greeted warmly, but Lindbergh returned unimpressed by what he had seen. A story that appeared in a London mimeographed newsheet titled *The Week* alleged that Lindbergh had informed members of "the Cliveden Set" (a pejorative term coined by *The Week* to characterize Lord and Lady Astor and their circle as Nazi sympathizers) that "the German air force could take on and defeat, single handed, the British, French, Soviet and Czechoslovakian air fleets." Although the article in *The Week* generally misrepresented the facts, *Pravda* reprinted the piece, and it was interpreted as factual. The Russian government branded Lindbergh a liar, the Soviet pilots he had befriended denounced him, and his hosts from the Russian embassy called for him to provide an accurate account of his visit, which he refused to do.

After his return to the United States in April 1939, Lindbergh went to visit General Henry H. "Hap" Arnold, who had been favorably impressed with his estimates of German air power, at West Point. As Arnold requested, Lindbergh entered active duty as a colonel in the U.S. Army Air Corps and began to assess American aircraft design and production. In May he made a three-week tour, inspecting aircraft production plants, aeronautical laboratories, airfields, and other essential installations. In addition, Lindbergh's influence on a board chaired by Brigadier General Walter G. Kilner, whose charge was to propose priorities in Army Air Corps research and development, was significant. Finally, Lindbergh gave much time and effort to the National Advisory Committee for Aeronautics, serving as chair of a committee devoted to the NACA and the aeronautical research facilities of universities in the United States.

Beginning in September 1939, Lindbergh actively took up the cause of American neutrality, making provocative speeches against involvement in European affairs, and provoking further criticism. His first speech on behalf of American nonintervention, "American and European Wars," took place on September 15, two weeks after Germany had invaded Poland, at the Carlton Hotel in Washington, D.C., and was carried to a national audience on the National Broadcasting System and the Columbia Broadcasting System. In it, Lindbergh argued that entering a European war was not in the best interests of the United States, and that the country should never enter a war unless it were "absolutely essential to the future welfare of the nation . . . . These wars in Europe are not wars in which our civilization is defending itself against some Asiatic intruder. There is no Genghis Khan or Xerxes." Lindbergh warned against propaganda: "We must learn to look behind every article we read and every speech we hear. We must not only inquire about the writer and the speaker—about his personal interests and nationality, but we must ask who owns and who influences the newspaper, the news picture, and the radio station." Lindbergh stressed that the United States did not have to enter the war to protect herself because of the oceans at either coast, and, moreover, that involvement would become permanent. These were the points that Lindbergh would continually hammer home in his speeches on nonintervention over the course of some twenty-seven months until America's entry into the war in December 1941. The speech was controversial, and newspapers and commentators criticized it. Syndicated columnist Dorothy Thompson was especially disparaging, calling it the product of a "pro-Nazi recipient of a German medal."[32]

A short time later, Lindbergh created still more controversy. In a November 1939 article in *Reader's Digest* titled "Aviation, Geography, and Race," and, later, in a March 1940 article in the *Atlantic Monthly* titled "What Substitute for War," he proclaimed aviation as a "tool specially shaped for Western hands, a scientific art which others only copy in a mediocre fashion, another barrier between the teeming millions of Asia and the Grecian inheritance of Europe—one of those priceless possessions which permit the White race to live at all in a pressing sea of Yellow, Black, and Brown. . . . It is time to turn from our quarrels and to build our White ramparts again. . . . It is our turn to guard our heritage from Mongol and Persian and Moor. . . . [Our civilization depends] on a united strength among ourselves; on a strength too great for foreign armies to challenge; on a Western Wall of race and arms which can hold back either a Genghis Khan or the infiltration of inferior blood; on an English fleet, a German air force, a French army, an American nation, standing together as guardians of our common heritage, sharing strength, dividing influence."[33]

Historian Albert Fried speculates that Lindbergh's thinking was motivated less by Nazi ideology than by his hatred of the Soviet Union and Communism.

Lindbergh (right)
and Juan Trippe of
Pan American Airways
stand on an early
Pan American clipper.
Lindbergh had consulted
for the company in the
1930s, but when he
approached Trippe
for a position during
World War II, he
was turned down.

Lindbergh, Fried writes, "did not have to spell out what he was driving at, the fact that Germany needed to dominate Europe, whether or not Britain or France liked it. Nor did he conceal his sympathy for this happy verdict of history. Germany, not the 'democracies' was facing the 'Asiatic hordes'; and Germany was occupying the 'intangible eastern border of European civilization,' as indeed she had done for thousands of years. But the threat from the east had never been so great, thanks to the Soviet Union and Communism. The possibility that the 'democracies' might be defeated did not in the least disturb Lindbergh's equanimity. Nor should it disturb America's in his view. If anything, he would welcome it as the triumph of nature over debilitation and loss of nerve."[34]

Readers who thought they saw similarities between Lindbergh's sentiments in "Aviation, Geography, and Race" and Nazi ideology were disturbed enough to write to FBI director J. Edgar Hoover and President Franklin D. Roosevelt demanding that the authorities keep a close watch on Lindbergh's activities and that he not be given access to important aviation information or entrusted with a position of authority in the federal government. At the least, this piece, together with Anne's book *The Wave of the Future,* published in the fall of 1940, made the Lindberghs susceptible to charges of promoting racist sentiment.

By late 1939, Lindbergh had come to be considered the most controversial exponent of nonintervention in the United States. Thus, it was not unexpected when he joined the America First Committee in April 1941. America First, founded in September 1940, had grown from a student organization at Yale University led by R. Douglas Stuart, Jr., a young law student and son of the first vice president of the Quaker Oats Company. It appeared as though national policy was moving in the direction of intervention in the wake of FDR's decision to run for a third term, the German invasion of Denmark, Norway, Belgium, and the Netherlands, and the fall of France. Roosevelt had encouraged the activities of interventionist groups, the most prominent of which were the Committee to Defend America by Aiding the Allies, a pro-British pressure group organized in May 1940, headed by William Allen White, editor of the *Emporia Gazette,* and Fight for Freedom, Inc., organized in April 1941, whose national chairman was the Episcopal bishop Henry W. Hobson of Ohio. In response to the growing interventionist movement, the America First Committee began to organize local chapters and mobilize a national effort. General Robert E. Wood, chairman of the board of Sears Roebuck & Company, was the America First Committee's national chairman and Stuart was national director. Among its members were the journalist John T. Flynn, the novelist Kathleen Norris, the wives of two U.S. Senators, Mrs. Bennett Champ Clark and Mrs. Burton K. Wheeler, the humorist Irvin S. Cobb, and former World War I combat ace Eddie Rickenbacker, who was chief of Eastern Air Transport.

Lindbergh's stance on nonintervention and his taking up of the cause of America First widened the rift between him and the Roosevelt administration. The origins of Lindbergh's antipathy to Franklin D. Roosevelt went back to February 9, 1934, after the president had cancelled private airmail contracts and ordered the Army Air Corps to fly the mail. Roosevelt also trumpeted rumors (later proven to be false) of fraud and collusion in the airline industry. Lindbergh rashly sent off an inflammatory 275-word telegram to the White House, claiming that the president had condemned the commercial aviation industry without due process of law. Lindbergh also sent a copy of the telegram to the morning papers, angering the administration, which felt that Lindbergh was seeking to discredit its motives and that he had a great deal to gain from the publicity, being who he was, and particularly because he was so intimately associated with Pan American Airways and Transcontinental Air Transport, two of the major U.S. airlines. Lindbergh's telegram worked in his favor. In an editorial, the *New York Times* took the Roosevelt administration to task and commented: "Here was a man Lindbergh, who could not be held up to scorn as a mere tool of corrupt and privileged interests." The President eventually relented, after the air corps had experienced some initial aircraft accidents and pilot deaths. Lindbergh had won this battle, but he would eventually pay the price for his disagreement with Roosevelt.[35]

Early in 1941, Lindbergh displeased the administration again by testifying before congressional committees against Roosevelt's proposed Lend-Lease Bill. This legislation would empower the president to provide war matériel to any country that was considered vital to the interests of the United States. Roosevelt, at a press conference in April 1941, when asked why the army, badly in need of pilots, had not recalled Lindbergh to service, likened the aviator to Clement L. Vallandigham, leader of the "Copperheads," Yankees who were sympathetic to the Confederate cause during the Civil War. Lindbergh saw this as an assault on his character and promptly resigned his commission as a colonel in the U.S. Army Air Corps Reserve. Harold Ickes, secretary of the interior and the FDR administration's principal spokesman in opposition to Lindbergh, added insult to injury by writing that Lindbergh had "returned his commission with suspicious alacrity and with a total lack of graciousness. But he still hangs on to the Nazi medal!"[36]

Meanwhile, another American hero, Alvin C. York—the celebrated Sergeant York of World War I fame—had taken issue with Lindbergh's and America First's position on America's intervention in the European war. York had distinguished himself by leading a group of American infantrymen who captured 132 German soldiers near Châtel-Chehèry in the Meuse-Argonne in October 1918. As the official spokesman for the Veterans of Foreign Wars, York began his attack on Lindbergh in a 1941 Memorial Day speech at the Tomb of the Unknown Soldier at Arlington National Cemetery. Among those in the audience was President Roosevelt. York said he was proud to be a member of the VFW, but stated disingenuously that the organization "could have chosen many far better speakers. There is a transatlantic aviator for one. And a United States Senator [Burton K. Wheeler] whose favorite bird must be the ostrich. They would have been glad to come here; but I was invited instead." Later in the speech, he indirectly criticized Lindbergh's contention that a negotiated settlement of the conflict in Europe would be in the best interests of everyone concerned.[37]

York continued to disparage Lindbergh's opinions on nonintervention. In a speech to the Tennessee Society of New York on July 3, 1941, he said that he would be sorry if Russia were defeated quickly (Germany had invaded the Soviet Union on June 22) "for a number of reasons. The first is Hitler *must* be stopped. The second is that a long, drawn out war between Russia and Germany would weaken both dictators. The third, and most important reason for my sorrow at a speedy German victory is that it will give fuel to such isolationists and appeasers as Senator Wheeler and ex-Colonel Lindbergh, and ex-President Hoover." As York's speech went on, Lindbergh became its chief target: "Can ex-Colonel Lindbergh now say that appeasement hasn't been given every conceivable chance to prove itself?" York went on to say that he had tried to understand Lindbergh's feelings, but had "failed in that . . . because of the fact that of all the medals I was fortunate enough to get, none of them came with the personal blessings of Adolf Hitler." York even went so far as to label Lindbergh a traitor and a coward because he had become so familiar with Nazi leaders during his tours of the aviation facilities in Germany during the late 1930s and because he had forsaken the United States for England, and subsequently refused to support his newly adopted county, which had welcomed him and his family in their time of need.[38]

The controversy concerning Lindbergh came to a head at an America First Committee rally at Des Moines, Iowa, in September 1941, where Lindbergh delivered a famous (or infamous) speech. In it he charged that the British, the Jews, and the Roosevelt administration were propelling the United States toward war. He contended that the Jews' "greatest danger to this country lies in their large ownership and influence in our motion pictures, our press, our radio, and our Government." For this Lindbergh was criticized roundly by interventionists and noninterventionists, Protestants, Catholics, and Jews, Republicans and Democrats, and even the Communist Party. He was again branded a pro-Nazi and an anti-Semite. Typical of the censure Lindbergh received was that of John T. Flynn, himself an America First Committee member. He wrote to Lindbergh that it was one thing to criticize bias in the press, "but this is a far different matter from going out on the public platform and denouncing 'the Jews' as war makers. No man can do that without incurring the guilt of religious and racial intolerance which is poison in a community like ours."[39]

Lindbergh's Des Moines speech effectively put an end to the America First Committee movement, but the noninterventionists had been steadily losing ground because it was becoming increasingly evident that the United States would be drawn into the war in one way or another. The Japanese attack on Pearl Harbor on December 7, 1941, made the controversy moot, but it left Lindbergh with what appeared to be a permanent stain. According to Lindbergh biographer Scott Berg, "other members of America First would bear no stigma for having been allied with that particular cause. But America First quickly entered the annals of public discourse tainted; and Charles Lindbergh would thenceforth be contaminated, considered by many wrong-headed at best and traitorous at worst."[40]

Nevertheless, Lindbergh offered his services to the Army Air Corps. He faced considerable opposition from the Roosevelt administration. Secretary of War Henry L. Stimson advised him that he was "unwilling to place in command of our troops as a commissioned officer any man who had such a lack of faith in our cause, as he had shown in his speeches." An arrangement with the War Department could have been worked out had Lindbergh been willing to retract his prewar views. Lindbergh, however, informed Assistant Secretary of War for Air Robert Lovett that he had no intention of doing so, and that effectively ended the matter.[41]

Lindbergh then made overtures to Juan Trippe at Pan American Airways and Guy Vaughan at Curtiss-Wright in regard to a civilian position on behalf of the war effort, but ultimately was told that there was considerable administration opposition to the idea. Both President Roosevelt and Secretary of the Interior Harold Ickes continued to distrust Lindbergh, despite the fact that the FBI's investigation of his activities which had begun in late 1939, had ended. In a letter to Roosevelt, Ickes left no doubt that he thought Lindbergh was a threat to national security: "To accept Lindbergh's offer would be to grant this loyal friend of Hitler's a precious opportunity on a golden platter," he wrote. "It would, in my opinion, be a tragic disservice to American democracy to give one of its bitterest and most ruthless enemies a chance to gain a military record. I ardently hope that this convinced fascist will not be given the opportunity to wear the uniform of the United States. . . . He should be buried in merciful oblivion."[42]

Lindbergh also met with Eugene Wilson, president of the United Aircraft Corporation, and Reuben Fleet of Consolidated Aircraft Corporation, to offer his services as a civilian. While both men were eager to hire him, no offer was forthcoming because of political considerations. Finally, at Henry Ford's invitation, Lindbergh went to work as a technical consultant on B-24 Liberator bomber production at Willow Run, near Ypsilanti, Michigan. While at Willow Run, he alternated between the B-24 work and high-altitude experiments at the Aeromedical

Opposite:

In 1942 Lindbergh performed tests in a high-altitude chamber at the Aeromedical Unit for Research in Aviation Medicine at the Mayo Clinic in Rochester, Minnesota.

During World War II Lindbergh was a technical representative for United Aircraft Corporation in the Pacific Theater. Here he is pictured in the cockpit of a Vought F4U Corsair, in which he tested emergency procedures for high-altitude flying.

Unit for Research in Aviation Medicine at the Mayo Clinic in Rochester, Minnesota. Then, as a technical representative of United Aircraft, Lindbergh went to the South Pacific to test the F4U Corsair and the P-38. At war's end, and despite official disapproval, he had flown fifty unauthorized combat missions and was credited with shooting down a Japanese fighter. Along the way Lindbergh had made improvements to the B-24, devised fuel-saving flying techniques for the P-38, and revised emergency procedures in high-altitude flying for the Corsair.

In April 1945, after Roosevelt's death on April 12 and on the eve of Germany's unconditional surrender on May 8, Lindbergh, in his capacity as technical consultant for United Aircraft, was invited to go to Europe to study German developments in high-speed aircraft as part of a Naval Technical Commission. A few months later, as part of his mission, he visited Nordhausen in the Harz Mountains of central Germany, where the V-2 rockets were built by slave laborers. To get to Nordhausen, Lindbergh and his young naval officer companion, Lieutenant W. H. Uellendahl, had to go through Camp Dora, which was part of the Nazi concentration camp at Bergen-Belsen. It was there that Lindbergh realized the atrocities committed by the Third Reich. In his wartime journals, he wrote: "Here was a place where men and life and death had reached the lowest form of degradation. How could any reward in national progress even faintly justify the establishment and operation of such a place. When the value of life and the dignity of death are removed, what is left for man?"[43]

Earlier, upon his visit to Berchtesgaden, Hitler's mountain retreat in the Bavarian Alps, Lindbergh had written in his journal: "Hitler . . . a man who controlled such power, who might have turned it to human good, who used it to such re-

Lindbergh poses with pilots on Emirau Island in the South Pacific in mid-1944.

sulting evil: the best youth of his country dead; the cities destroyed; the population homeless and hungry; Germany overrun by the forces he feared most, the forces of Bolshevism, the armies of Soviet Russia; much of his country, like his own room and quarters, rubble—flame-blacked ruins. I think of the strength of prewar Germany." Although he may have had second thoughts about his misjudgment of Hitler and Hitler's Germany, Lindbergh never acknowledged, either during his trip to Nordhausen or anytime later, that he had misjudged Hitler and Nazi Germany. Anne Morrow Lindbergh would later write that "the worst crimes of the Nazis were not known until after Pearl Harbor and some not until the end of the war or even until the Nuremberg Trials;" nevertheless, she admitted that she and her husband "were both very blind, especially in the beginning, to the worst evils of the Nazi system."[44]

In *Under a Wing,* a touching memoir about her family, Lindbergh's daughter Reeve, probed deeply into the conundrum of her father's beliefs during the 1930s and 1940s. She was "transfixed and horrified" by the Des Moines speech. "I felt a global anguish—the horror of the Holocaust, the words of my own father ignoring the horror, but surely not condoning the horror, surely not dismissing, or diminishing it, surely not. But I also felt a piercingly personal rage . . . . There was no question in my mind about what my father was saying, or its implications. What I really wanted to know was, what did he *think* he was saying? Did he really believe that he was simply, dispassionately 'stating the facts,' as he later persistently claimed, without understanding that the very framework of the statement reverberated with anti-Semitic resonance? And if he really believed what he believed, and really did not understand what he did not understand, was that in itself not a form, however innocent he might think it, of anti-Semitism? Was there, in fact, such a thing as innocent, unconscious anti-Semitism? Was it prevalent before the war, and did the Holocaust forever criminalize an attitude that was previously acceptable and widespread among the non-Jewish population of this country and others?" Ultimately, she wants to know "how could someone who spoke the words my father did in 1941, never repudiating or amending them for the rest of his life, how did such a person raise children who, by his instruction and his example, day after day and year after year, had learned from him—not simply from our mother, but from him too—that such words were repellent and unspeakable? How did that happen, and what did it mean, not just for my own family but for others? And there are, indeed, many others who struggle as I do with the words spoken and written by past generations, words left by the very people whom they have most loved and respected, words they cannot accept."[45]

A smiling Lindbergh relaxes during a 1968 trip to Baja, California. It was in the 1960s that the pilot became involved in environmental causes.

AFTER THE WAR, Lindbergh's reputation, which had suffered a great deal as a result of his America First activity and the perception of his anti-Semitism, was rehabilitated. Ironically, his hatred and suspicion of the Soviet Union, which may have been instrumental in motivating him before the war, became a badge of honor in the postwar period. As Walter Hixson points out, "whereas Lindbergh's opposition to U.S. intervention had made him an outsider from 1939 to 1941, his uncompromising anticommunism and support for increased American military power became mainstream views in the Cold War." In 1954, at the suggestion of Secretary of the Air Force Harold Talbott, President Dwight D. Eisenhower essentially restored Lindbergh's commission, and he was made a brigadier general in the Air Force Reserve. He spent a considerable amount of time as an advisor to the Strategic Air Command and member of the Air Force Scientific Advisory Board, as well as serving on a congressionally created commission to select a permanent site for the U.S. Air Force Academy. He also continued to work for Pan American Airways.[46]

But there had been a profound change in his priorities. Although he was still active in aviation, Lindbergh had come to question it and to reflect on its ultimate value. His interest in things scientific and technological gradually gave way to a concern for the fragile planet and the spiritual development of mankind in a world of materialistic values. The first sign of this transition was the publication of his book *Of Flight and Life* in 1948. In it he wrote: "I have seen the science I worshipped, and the aircraft I loved, destroying the civilization I expected them to serve, and which I thought as permanent as the earth itself. In memory, the vision of my mailplane boring northward over moonlit clouds is now mingled with the streaks of tracers from my fighter, flaming comets of warplanes, and bombs falling irretrievably through the air."[47]

This perspective is also evident in his acceptance address on being awarded the Daniel Guggenheim Medal in 1953 "For Pioneering Achievements in Flight and Air Navigation." In it, Lindbergh said, "When the art of flying was young, most of us thought that men on wings would soar over mountains and oceans to bring countries close together in peaceful understanding. . . . Now at the end of the first half-century of engine-driven flight, we are confronted with the stark fact that the historical significance of aircraft has been primarily military and destructive. . . . Aviation is having its greatest effect on the force-influence of nations and factors of survival, while diplomatic relationships are floundering in a strange new framework of power, time, and space."[48]

Susan Gray sees the transition in Lindbergh's life as a consequence of World War II. Gray contends that the effects of the war "on the national character were reflected also in Lindbergh's own development; his attitudes toward aviation, science, and progress in general shifted radically from the faith and optimism which had marked his outlook ten to twenty years earlier. . . . He began to see clearly some of the goals to which he had devoted himself, and he began to reevaluate these goals. The direct manifestations of reevaluation were seen most particularly in his reaffirmation of the values of the natural world, in a recognition of the mystical and reli-

gious aspects of life, and in the increased emphasis which he put on a state of existence in which all the elements of life were to be kept in balance."[49]

In 1964, Lindbergh joined the board of directors of the World Wildlife Fund.
His interest in environmental causes began in the early 1960s when he lived with
Maasai tribespeople in East Africa, a region he visited at least ten times throughout
the course of the decade. During this period of his life Lindbergh became interested
in saving the blue and humpbacked whales that were being slaughtered off the coast
of Peru, and the tamarau (a wild buffalo) and the monkey-eating eagle of the
Philippines. Another indication of Lindbergh's shift of priorities was his position on
the development of the American SST (supersonic transport). On behalf of Pan
American, Lindbergh had been involved in planning with two SST design groups—

In his later years
Lindbergh became
increasingly concerned
with conservation, nature,
and the environment. In
June 1967 he went on an
expedition to Udjung Kulon,
a game preserve in
Indonesia, home of the last
remaining Javan rhinos.

a French-English consortium working on the Concorde and an American group overseen by the Federal Aviation Administration. He became opposed to the idea on economic and environmental grounds, and it is believed that his opposition to American development of such an aircraft was largely responsible for its defeat in the U.S. Senate in 1971. As Leonard S. Reich intimates in the title of his article on Lindbergh's transformation to environmental advocate—"From the Spirit of St. Louis to the SST"— Lindbergh had come a long way from the optimism about aviation that was embodied in the 1927 flights of the *Spirit of St. Louis,* and by the early 1970s his life and priorities had changed fundamentally.[50]

In light of the trajectory of Lindbergh's life it is not difficult to see why the *Spirit of St. Louis,* although an historically significant artifact, is mute when it comes to the question of Lindbergh's complexity and ambiguity as a human being. The aircraft represents a moment in time when the American people conferred on Lindbergh celebrity-heroic status. Another National Air and Space Museum artifact, the Lockheed Sirius *Tingmissartoq,* which the Lindberghs flew on pioneering flights to the Orient in 1931 and in search of commercial routes across the Atlantic in 1933, is perhaps more representative of Lindbergh because it tells us more about his aviation-building contributions. Ultimately, however, neither aircraft can shed more than cursory light on Lindbergh's identity.

Despite his immense influence on aviation, it is not certain that Lindbergh's substantial contributions—his technical expertise and his lifelong efforts toward placing American aviation on a sound footing both commercially and technologically—were ever fully comprehended by the American people. Moreover, his accomplishments in other areas of his life—his work with Alexis Carrel on a blood perfusion pump, his advocacy of environmental issues, his concern for regaining the spiritual values that he believed had been lost in a technological age—went largely unnoticed. In their search for a popular hero, the vast majority of Americans were concerned more with Lindbergh as celebrity or villain than with the pattern of his life.

Regardless of his multifaceted career, Lindbergh is still remembered largely as a pilot-hero. His mystique was an important aspect of the public's perception of aviation and aviators in the late 1920s and throughout the 1930s. After he had reached his goal, Lindbergh became an American idol of mythic proportions and his deed brought aviation and the idea of the pilot as hero firmly into the forefront of American consciousness. As so often happens, however, Americans' perception of Lindbergh soon became so overstated that it outstripped reality. Later, Lindbergh's celebrity as a hero made it all the more difficult for Americans to forgive his uncritical advocacy of Nazi Germany during the 1930s and his unpopular isolationist stand before World War II.

The question of Lindbergh's heroism remains. Was being heroic tied to a specific time and place; in other words, his transatlantic flight in the *Spirit of St. Louis* or the flights in the *Tingmissartoq?* Is Daniel Boorstin correct in his assessment that "Lindbergh's singularly impressive heroic deed was soon far overshadowed by his even more impressive publicity" and that "his stature as a hero was nothing compared to his stature as celebrity"? Was Lindbergh heroic in embracing environmental and humanitarian causes in the latter stages of his life? Does the controversy that surrounds him in regard to his outspokenness on the eve of World War II make him less heroic? These are questions for each generation of historians to answer for itself. Perhaps Dixon Wecter's assessment of what Americans value in their heroes holds true in the case of Lindbergh: "Hard work, tenacity, enterprise, and firmness in the face of odds are the qualities that Americans most admire, rather than originality or eloquence of tongue and pen." One might add that in America, "firmness in the face of odds" by the man of action is especially favored.[51]

Whatever one can say or not say about Lindbergh's heroism, it is impossible to dismiss the fact that in the course of his life Lindbergh transcended his original persona and played various roles—scientist, philosopher, literary man, naturalist, military man, among others—moving easily and successfully from one to another. Richard Hallion points out that there were many Lindberghs and that "his was the idealized existence of Renaissance Man; his temperament and restlessness did not permit him to develop a limited world view." Moreover, Kenneth Davis has argued that "no other contemporary life story, viewed psycho-historically, is richer than Lindbergh's in symbolic meaning and direct historical implication." Lindbergh, then, is paradigmatic of the man who struggles constantly to understand his historical and existential milieu, who questions his existence with every deed, and whose life is devoted to finding meaning in action.[52]

Whether we like or admire him or see him as heroic in the traditional sense would be of no consequence to Lindbergh, because as Davis points out, "Here, we feel, is a serious man. He remains unsatisfied by creature comforts and sensual pleasures. He rebels against that triviality of mind which advertising men generate as a prerequisite of mass purchasing and consumption. He demands to know *why*: he concerns himself with essential questions. No doubt they are questions which can never be finally answered in a continuously evolving universe, but they are nonetheless questions every human being must strive to answer if he would be truly human."[53]

The *Spirit* and the Smithsonian Institution

O N   M A Y   2 3 ,   1 9 2 7 , two days after Lindbergh landed in Paris, Secretary of the Smithsonian Charles G. Abbot had sent him a telegram, written by Paul E. Garber, the person responsible for the aviation collection, requesting the aircraft for the institution. Lindbergh readily agreed, but replied that the decision was not his, as he did not own the aircraft. So pleased were Harold Bixby and the rest of his backers, however, that they gave the *Spirit* to Lindbergh. With that, Lindbergh agreed to transfer the aircraft to the Smithsonian and thereby to the American people. His one stipulation was that it would come from all of his partners.

On April 30, 1928, the *Spirit of St. Louis* made its last flight. With Lindbergh at the controls one final time, the aircraft flew from St. Louis to Bolling Field in Washington, D.C., covering 725 miles with a brisk tailwind in four hours and fifty-eight minutes. The aircraft had completed 174 flights and stayed aloft for 489 hours and 28 minutes. Once in Washington, it was disassembled and towed carefully through the streets of the nation's capital during the early morning hours. It was re-assembled in the north hall of the Arts and Industries building of the National Museum. With the *Spirit* hanging prominently from steel cables in the ceiling, the new exhibit was opened to the public on Sunday, May 13, 1928, one week short of the first anniversary of Lindbergh's epic flight.

At first the aircraft was lent to the Smithsonian pending the clarification of legal technicalities and the final determination of the wishes of Lindbergh and his backers. Lindbergh understandably insisted that the aircraft always remain on display, as stated in the formal Deed of Conveyance, "with a degree of dignity, prominence, and accessibility to the public equal to the setting and circumstances now surrounding its exhibition by the Smithsonian Institution."[54] Lindbergh also insisted that the cockpit should always be visible to the public. One year later these details were settled, and on May 20, 1929, two years to the day after he took off from

Opposite:
Lindbergh wore this flight suit, helmet, and goggles while flying his Lockheed Sirius.

The *Spirit of St. Louis* arrives at the Smithsonian Institution on May 13, 1928. The plane was towed through the streets of Washington, D.C. from nearby Bolling Field.

Roosevelt Field, Lindbergh and his partners sold the *Spirit of St. Louis* to the Smithsonian for the sum of one dollar.

The museum took great care in protecting the aircraft. A proper exhibit was created beneath the aircraft, which hung securely just beyond the reach of the inquisitive public. In order to preserve the original markings, the museum's staff applied a coat of clear varnish over the aluminum cowling. Unfortunately, they did not realize the extent to which the varnish would yellow with age. As a result, the *Spirit of St. Louis* has developed a golden hue on its cowling.

Almost immediately after the *Spirit* was received by the National Museum, the Smithsonian and Lindbergh were besieged by requests to borrow the aircraft. Ten years after the donation, Lindbergh sent Dr. Abbot a letter on December 8, 1939, expressing his desire that the *Spirit* never leave the Smithsonian. In it, Lindbergh clearly stated, "I would like to have a record in your files of my opposition to moving the plane to any other location for temporary exhibition regardless of who makes

Smithsonian Secretary Charles G. Abbot stands before the *Spirit* during the aircraft's installation.

The *Spirit* was suspended from the ceiling in the North Hall of the Smithsonian's Arts and Industries Building from 1928 until 1975.

the request or how worthy the cause may be." To this day requests are still made but are always turned down.[55]

The *Spirit of St. Louis* remained untouched until 1948, when the Smithsonian took possession of the original 1903 Wright Flyer from Orville Wright. With little room left in the Arts and Industries building and no room left in the Aircraft Building of the recently formed National Air Museum, Smithsonian officials decided to place the world's first successful aircraft in the north hall. This meant moving the *Spirit* back from its prominent position near the entrance. Concerned officials contacted Lindbergh to discern his opinion and were relieved when he gave his enthusiastic blessing. He felt honored to have his aircraft displayed behind history's most significant aircraft.

Occasionally Lindbergh would visit the museum and his faithful airplane. When Lindbergh was preparing the manuscript for his Pulitzer Prize-winning book *The Spirit of St. Louis,* he wanted to inspect his aircraft one more time. Paul Garber arranged for a ladder and for almost an hour Lindbergh sat inside his famous aircraft reflecting and taking notes as he relived his many experiences.

The *Spirit of St. Louis* remained in its place of honor in the Arts and Industries building until 1975. With the opening of the new National Air and Space Museum scheduled for July 1, 1976, it was time to move all of the aircraft from the old building and out to the Silver Hill restoration facility for a thorough examination. While at the "Hill," the aircraft was carefully vacuumed and small tears in the fabric repaired. The fabric was hand washed with a mild detergent solution and all of the metal was treated with preservative, and visible rust removed. The fragile tires were treated with silicone and the delicate wicker seat cleaned and treated with linseed oil. The propeller was removed, cleaned, and treated to prevent corrosion, as was the hub. The engine was dusted and cleaned by hand. The spark plugs were removed and treated with preservative, as were the cylinders. Once reinstalled, the propeller was turned by hand to ensure that the preservative was distributed throughout the engine. An examination inside one rockerbox revealed that the trusty Wright Whirlwind was still well protected by its oil.

The inspection of the *Spirit* went well, but the public grew restless awaiting its return. As a result, the museum placed the aircraft on display in the new building several months before the official opening. When the new National Air and Space Museum did open, the public was able to see the refurbished *Spirit of St. Louis* in its magnificent new setting. It could also see inside the cockpit better than before.

In the intervening years, the museum was also able to collect several original parts

During the refurbishment of the Milestones of Flight gallery in 2000 and 2001, the *Spirit of St. Louis* was temporarily located in the west end of the National Air and Space Museum.

from the aircraft. In 1971 Stanley Vaughan donated the cracked propeller shroud that Curtiss mechanics replaced just before the transatlantic flight. In 1989, the family of Harvey Bowlus gave the original spinner cap with the names of all of the people who had built the *Spirit of St. Louis* painted inside it. All questions of authenticity were answered when the two pieces were fitted together perfectly. These items and Lindbergh's survival kit, which was donated by Ryan and *Spirit of St. Louis* historian Ev Cassagneres, remain on display next to the aircraft to this day.

For years the *Spirit* enthralled millions of visitors to the National Air and Space Museum. While the aircraft appeared to be in fine shape, staff members grew concerned with the possibility of internal corrosion, especially at the engine mounts. The aircraft had never received an internal inspection and the thought of the engine or another part of the aircraft falling to the gallery floor was too frightening to comprehend. While plans were underway in 1991 to determine when this inspection could take place, events hastened the decision.

During a routine gallery inspection, an attentive security officer noticed a growing tear in the fabric along the top of the *Spirit*'s fuselage near the rear hanging point. It looked as though the aircraft's structure was failing. Quickly the officer reported this to the curator and soon the museum leapt into action to preserve one of its most valuable artifacts.

On January 23, 1992, the skilled restoration technicians of the museum's Paul E. Garber facility, under the direction of foreman William Reese, carefully released the *Spirit* and brought it cautiously down to the floor of the Milestones of Flight gallery. There, for the next two months, they and experts from the Smithsonian's Conservation Analytical Laboratory inspected every inch of the aircraft.

To the relief of all, it was discovered that a broken wooden stringer had caused the torn fabric in the rear fuselage. The steel tube fuselage was sound. Apparently, when the aircraft was resuspended in the mid–1970s, the rear support cable had been wrapped around the pivot point of the tail skid. Over time, the rubber bushing—or lining—inside the skid dried up, causing the cable to slip a fraction of an inch, enough to crack the stringer and tear the fabric. Fortunately, the aircraft had never been at risk. Nevertheless, when the *Spirit* was rehung, the cable was installed in a more satisfactory location.

The Conservation Analytical Laboratory was enlisted to employ X-ray techniques to examine the steel airframe of the *Spirit*. It was feared that water trapped inside the steel tubing might have reacted with air and caused unseen rust, thereby weakening the airframe and engine mount. An X-ray examination of the steel revealed the contrary. The welders at Ryan knew their craft: each tube had been properly heated by a blowtorch, evaporating the air inside the steel tubing before the welds were made. There was no rust found anywhere on the aircraft. The airframe was almost as good as new. Furthermore, testing of the engine mounts revealed that they were carrying only one-twelfth of the maximum weight they could tolerate. The five-hundred-pound Wright Whirlwind was on to stay.

The *Spirit* was again thoroughly cleaned and the small fabric tears repaired. In addition, the yellowed and crazed skylight was replaced by a tinted Plexiglas panel. The original was then placed into climate-controlled storage. With the repairs and inspections completed, a Plexiglas panel was installed over the doorway to keep out dust but allow visitors to see inside the cockpit, as Lindbergh wished. On the evening of March 25, 1992, the *Spirit of St. Louis* was carefully lifted back into place and attached to a new set of steel cables.

On a personal note, Bob van der Linden can attest to the excellent condition of the *Spirit of St. Louis*. Early one morning he arrived at work and observed a lighting technician replacing a fixture above the *Spirit*. The technician was reaching from the basket of a powered lift. Before he had a chance to say anything he heard a nervous "oops" and saw a wrench falling in slow motion toward the right wing of the aircraft. With visions of a severely damaged wing rushing through his head he saw the wrench strike the wing and, to his astonishment, bounce harmlessly to the floor. A closer examination revealed no damage to the seventy-year-old fabric or the structure of the wing.

Recently, because of repairs to the windows of the museum, the *Spirit of St. Louis* was temporarily removed from the Milestones of Flight gallery. On Halloween 2000, the experienced crew of NASM restoration specialists once again removed the aircraft from its post. It was then slowly and carefully moved along the floor to the west gallery and resuspended above the Wright Flyer. In its new location the *Spirit* was installed in a dramatic climbing attitude and was visible along the entire length of the second-floor balcony. Though spectacular in its temporary location, it was returned to its place of honor high above in the Milestones of Flight gallery when the gallery reopened in 2001.

Since 1928 the Smithsonian has been the proud keeper of Charles Lindbergh's *Spirit of St. Louis,* making it available for millions of visitors to see each year. It is one of the most popular artifacts at the National Air and Space Museum and will continue to draw huge crowds for decades to come, since it represents a unique accomplishment of a remarkable man and his remarkable machine.

LIST OF SUPPLIERS AND MANUFACTURERS

The following companies contributed parts and materials to the *Spirit of St. Louis*.

AIRFRAME

Steel tubing	Ohio Seamless Company, Shelby, Ohio
Steel tubing (chrome molybdenum)	Summerill Tube Company, Bridgeport, Pa.
Steel tubing	Service Steel Company, Los Angeles
Alloy steels	Crucible Steel Company of America, New York
Aluminum sheet metal and tubing	Aluminum Company of America (ALCOA), San Francisco
Steel sheet metal	Dickerson Steel Company, Dayton, Ohio
Fabrics, tapes, etc.	E. S. Twining Company, New York
Dope, dope thinner	Brown-Leithold Company, Los Angeles
Varnish	Valentine and Company, New York
Lacquer, bronze, enamel	W. P. Fuller Company, San Diego
Metal primer, varnish	Bass Hueter Company, Los Angeles
Spruce, ash, black walnut	Sullivan Hardwood Company, San Diego
Spruce	Posey and Company, Portland, Oreg.
Mahogany plywood	California Plywood and Veneer, Los Angeles
Plywood	Haskelite Manufacturing Company, Chicago
Balsawood	Fleischmann Transportation Company, New York
Cottonwood plywood	White Brothers, San Francisco
Celluloid, upholstering	Henry D. Day, Company, Los Angeles
Glue, waterproof	Hercules Glue Company, San Francisco
Fasteners, "Lift-the-Dot"	Carr Fastener Company, Cambridge, Mass.
Tires and innertubes (Silvertown Cords)	B. F. Goodrich Company, San Diego
Wheels	Dayton Wire Wheel Company, Dayton, Ohio
Bolts, nuts and accessories	Nicholas-Beazley Airplane Company, Marshall, Mo.
Accessories	Johnson Airplane Company, Dayton, Ohio
Wires and fittings	Roeblings and Sons, Los Angeles
Gasoline lines and fittings	Lunkenheimer Company, Cincinnati, Ohio
Tanks, gasoline and oil, aluminum cowling	Standard Sheet Metal Works, San Diego
Hose clamps	Ideal Hose Clamp Company, Brooklyn, N.Y.
Propeller	Standard Steel Propeller Company, Pittsburgh, Pa.
Raft and oars	Airships Inc., Hammondsport, N.Y.
Armburst Life Saving Cup	C. W. Armburst, Washington, D.C.

ENGINE AND ENGINE ACCESSORIES

Engine	Wright Aeronautical Corporation, Paterson, N.J.
Magnetos, Model AG-9D	Scintilla Aircraft Magneto Company, Sidney, N.Y.
Carburetor	Stromberg Motor Devices Company, Chicago
Spark plugs	A. C. Spark Plug Company, Flint, Mich.

INSTRUMENTS

Air speed indicator	Pioneer Instrument Company, Brooklyn, N.Y.
Compass, magnetic	Pioneer Instrument Company, Brooklyn, N.Y.
Compass, earth inductor	Pioneer Instrument Company, Brooklyn, N.Y.
Speed and drift meter	Pioneer Instrument Company, Brooklyn, N.Y.
Turn-and-bank indicator	Pioneer Instrument Company, Brooklyn, N.Y.
Inclinometer	Pioneer Instrument Company, Brooklyn, N.Y.
Speed timer	Pioneer Instrument Company, Brooklyn, N.Y.
Jones tachometer	Consolidated Instrument Company, N.Y.
Motometer	Moto-Meter Company, Long Island, N.Y.
Clock, eight day	Waltham National Watch Company, Waltham, Mass.
Econometer	Charles Lindbergh (built by Ryan Airlines, San Diego)
Oil Pressure Gauge	U. S. War Department stock

FUEL AND OIL

Gasoline	Standard Oil of California
Oil	Vacuum Oil Company, New York

Source: *Aviation*, June 20, 1927, p. 1,370

Of the major vendors for the *Spirit of St. Louis*, the following companies still exist in either their original form or as part of another company:

1927	2002
B. F. Goodrich Company	B. F. Goodrich Company
Vacuum Oil Company	Exxon Mobil
Standard Oil of California	Chevron
Aluminum Company of America	Aluminum Company of America
Wright Aeronautical Corporation	Curtiss-Wright Corporation
A. C. Spark Plug Company	ACDelco
Standard Steel Propeller Company	Hamilton Sundstrand, formerly known as Hamilton Standard
Pioneer Instrument Company	Honeywell, formerly known as Bendix

Ryan Airlines, the builder of the *Spirit of St. Louis*, no longer exists. Soon after Lindbergh's flight in July 1927, the company changed its name to the B. F. Mahoney Aircraft Corporation. In 1928, Mahoney sold control of his company to Harold Bixby and Harry Knight and moved the company to St. Louis again changing its name to the Mahoney Aircraft Corporation. Mahoney remained on as president and in July 1928, the company was renamed the Mahoney-Ryan Aircraft Corporation thus taking advantage of the marketing opportunities made available by linking the company to Lindbergh and the old Ryan Airlines.

In late 1928 and early 1929, the stock market boomed as aviation matured as a business and industry consolidations quickly occurred. By the spring of 1929 most aircraft manufacturers, airlines, and suppliers had been swept up into large holding companies. In May 1929, the Detroit Aircraft Corporation acquired Mahoney-Ryan and promptly renamed its new subsidiary the Ryan Aircraft Corporation. However less than two years later, as the Great Depression approached, the Detroit Aircraft Corporation and its Ryan subsidiary closed their doors permanently.

T. Claude Ryan had sold his interest in Ryan Airlines to B. F. Mahoney in November 1926. While Ryan initially stayed for a few months as general manager, he soon left. In April 1929 Claude Ryan purchased what was left of his old factory in San Diego and formed a new company, the T. C. Ryan Aeronautical Corporation. In 1969 he sold his firm to Teledyne thereby creating Teledyne Ryan which still exists today.

NOTES

1. Kenneth Davis, *The Hero: Charles A. Lindbergh and the American Dream* (Garden City, New York: Doubleday & Company, 1959), 18.

2. Charles A. Lindbergh, *The Spirit of St. Louis* (New York: Charles Scribner's Sons, 1953), 264–65.

3. Davis, 95. The accounts of Lindbergh's early flying experiences to which Davis refers are from Charles Lindbergh's *We: The Famous Flier's Own Story of His Life and Transatlantic Flight* (New York: G. P. Putnam's Sons), 1927, and Lindbergh's *The Spirit of St. Louis* (New York: Charles Scribner's Sons), 1953.

4. Charles Lindbergh, *Spirit*, 267–68.

5. Davis, 101.

6. Davis, 112. Caterpillar was the name given to the organization because caterpillars produce silk, the fabric from which parachutes were often made.

7. Davis, 116–17.

8. Quoted in A. Scott Berg, *Lindbergh* (New York: G. P. Putnam's Sons, 1998), 83-84; quoted in Davis, 129.

9. Charles Lindbergh, *Spirit*, 4.

10. Davis, 141.

11. Quoted in Berg, 292.

12. Quoted in Berg, 95.

13. "Lindbergh's Reception at Washington," *Current History* (July 1927): 529–30.

14. "Lindbergh's Reception in New York," *Current History* (July 1927): 531–32.

15. "Lindbergh's Reception in New York," *Current History* (July 1927): 532, 534.

16. Daniel Boorstin, *The Image: A Guide to Pseudo-Events in America* (New York: Atheneum, 1975), 68; Tom Wolfe, *The Right Stuff* (New York: Bantam Books, 1980), 117, italics Wolfe's.

17. The *New York Times*, May 23, 1927, 20.

18. Laurence Goldstein, "Lindbergh in 1927: The Response of Poets to the Poem of Fact," *Prospects* 5 (1980): 293–94.

19. Boorstin, 66, 68.

20. John William Ward, "The Meaning of Lindbergh's Flight," in *Studies in American Culture: Dominant Ideas and Images,* ed. Joseph J. Kwiat and Mary C. Turpie (Minneapolis, Minn.: University of Minnesota Press, 1960), 27–40.

21. R. E. G. Davies, *Airlines of the United States since 1914* (Washington, D.C.: Smithsonian Institution Press, 1972), 33.

22. Michael S. Sherry, *The Rise of American Air Power: The Creation of Armageddon* (New Haven, Conn.: Yale University Press, 1987), 41.

23. Davis, 253.

24. *New York Times* account quoted in Davis, 271; Dixon Wecter, *The Hero in America: A Chronicle of Hero Worship* (Ann Arbor, Mich.: University of Michigan Press, 1963), 439.

25. Davis, 265–66, italics Davis's.

26. According to Robert Hessen, ed., *Berlin Alert: The Memoirs and Reports of Truman Smith* (Stanford, Calif.: Hoover Institution Press, Stanford University, 1984), v. Lindbergh made five trips to Germany: July 22–August 2, 1936; October 11–25, 1937; October 11–29, 1938; December 1938 and January 1939.

27. Quoted in Berg, 356.

28. Quoted in Berg, 357.

29. Quoted in Berg, 359, 360–61; Walter L. Hixson, *Charles A. Lindbergh: Lone Eagle*, Library of American Biography, ed. Oscar Handlin (New York: Harper Collins College Publishers, 1996), 91.

30. Quoted in Berg, 368; Hessen, 114.

31. Quoted in Wayne S. Cole, *Charles A. Lindbergh and the Battle Against American Intervention in World War II* (New York: Harcourt Brace Jovanovich, 1974), 43; quoted in Berg, 381.

32. Quoted in Walter S. Ross, *The Last Hero: Charles A. Lindbergh*, rev. ed. (New York: Harper & Row) 296–97; quoted in Berg, 397.

33. Quoted in Berg, 394; quoted in Davis, 391-92.

34. Albert Fried, *FDR and His Enemies* (New York: Palgrave, 1999), 188.

35. *New York Times* account quoted in Davis, 334.

36. Quoted in Berg, 424.

37. Quoted in Michael E. Birdwell, *Celluloid Soldiers: The Warner Bros. Campaign against Nazism* (New York: New York University Press, 1999), 137.

38. Quoted in Birdwell, 139, 140.

39. Quoted in Cole, 171–72; quoted in Joyce Milton, *Loss of Eden: A Biography of Charles and Anne Morrow Lindbergh* (New York: HarperCollins Publishers, 1993), 401.

40. Berg, 433.

41. Quoted in Hixson, 115.

42. Quoted in Dorothy Herrmann, *Anne Morrow Lindbergh: A Gift for Life* (New York: Penguin Books, 1993), 266.

43. Quoted in Berg, 467–68.

44. Quoted in Berg, 465, 469.

45. Reeve Lindbergh, *Under A Wing: A Memoir* (New York: Delta, 1999), 201-02, 202-03, italics Lindbergh's.

46. Hixson, 122.

47. Quoted in Susan M. Gray, *Charles A. Lindbergh and the American Dilemma: The Conflict of Technology and Human Values* (Bowling Green, Ohio: Bowling Green State University Popular Press, 1988), 57. Gray provides a cogent analysis of Lindbergh's transition from material to spiritual values.

48. Charles A. Lindbergh, "Acceptance of Daniel Guggenheim Medal by Charles A. Lindbergh," in supplement to *Pioneering in Aeronautics* (New York: The Daniel Guggenheim Medal Board of Award, 1952), 7–8.

49. Gray, 55, 62–63.

50. Leonard S. Reich, "From the *Spirit of St. Louis* to the SST: Charles Lindbergh, Technology, and Environment," *Technology and Culture* (April 1995): 351–53.

51. Boorstin, 68; Wecter, 485.

52. Richard P. Hallion, "Charles A. Lindbergh and Aviation Technology," in *Charles A. Lindbergh: An American Life*, ed. Tom D. Crouch (Washington, D.C.: National Air and Space Museum, Smithsonian Institution, 1977), 39; Kenneth S. Davis, review of *Lindbergh: A Biography*, by Leonard Mosley, *New York Times Book Review*, April 11, 1976, 4.

53. Davis, 429, italics Davis's.

54. Deed of Conveyance, Ryan NY-P *Spirit of St. Louis*, May 20, 1929, Registrar's Files, National Air and Space Museum, Smithsonian Institution, Washington, D.C.

55. Charles A. Lindbergh to C. G. Abbot, December 8, 1939, Registrar's Files, National Air and Space Museum, Smithsonian Institution, Washington, D.C.

GLOSSARY

AIR SPEED INDICATOR. An instrument that shows the relative speed of an aircraft's movement through the air.

ALTIMETER. An instrument that indicates the altitude at which an aircraft is flying above sea level or a set reference level.

BAROGRAPH. An instrument that keeps a continuous record of barometric pressure; i.e., the pressure exerted by the earth's atmosphere at any given point, over a long period of time. The instrument records the pressure in non-freezing ink on a circular chart and is used to verify and authenticate record-setting or record-breaking flights.

CHORD. The straight line that runs through the centers of the curvature of the leading and trailing edges of an airfoil section, such as an aircraft wing; a wing's width or thickness.

CLARK Y AIRFOIL. A typical airfoil (a surface designed for movement through the air, such as a wing, rudder, or stabilizer) shape of the 1920s, developed by Virginius E. Clark, an engineer at McCook Field. The Clark Y is characterized by its thickness of chord and its flat undersurface.

DEAD RECKONING. A method of navigation by which one determines a position by keeping an account of the course and distance from a previously known position called the point of departure.

DRIFT METER. A hand-held instrument designed to measure the angle of an aircraft's drift. This information enables the pilot to make allowances for cross winds and to make adjustments to maintain a selected course.

EARTH INDUCTOR COMPASS. A compass that relies upon the current generated in a coil revolving in the earth's magnetic field for its indications of direction.

EMPENNAGE. A French term for the tail group of an aircraft comprised of the following four components:

> *Rudder.* A movable control surface designed to regulate an aircraft in yaw, or side-to-side motion.
> *Vertical Fin.* A fixed, vertical, auxiliary airfoil surface that provides an aircraft with directional stability.
> *Elevator.* A movable control surface designed to regulate an aircraft in pitch, or up-and-down movement.
> *Horizontal stabilizer.* A fixed horizontal tail plane.

I-BEAM SPAR WING. The main longitudinal member of the wing possessing a cross-section shaped like the letter "I."

INCLINOMETER. A device that indicates the relationship of the longitudinal axis of an aircraft to the horizontal axis. The instrument shows whether an aircraft's nose is on the horizon or pointing up or down.

LONGERON. The primary longitudinal part of an aircraft's fuselage or its main structural body.

PARASOL MONOPLANE. A single-wing aircraft in which the wing is positioned above the fuselage, or main structural body of the aircraft.

STILL AIR RANGE. The maximum distance an aircraft can fly in calm air.

TACHOMETER. An instrument that shows the revolutions per minute of an engine.

TURN-AND-BANK INDICATOR. Two instruments, one consisting of a steel ball, and another of an air bubble, which show whether an aircraft's wings are level in straight flight or properly inclined to turn.

WING LOADING. The gross weight of a fully loaded aircraft divided by the gross wing area.

BIBLIOGRAPHY

BOOKS

Allen, Peter C. *The 91 Before Lindbergh*. Shrewsbury, England: Airlife Publishers, 1985.

Berg, A. Scott. *Lindbergh*. New York: G. P. Putnam's Sons, 1998.

Birdwell, Michael E. *Celluloid Soldiers: The Warner Bros. Campaign against Nazism*. New York: New York University Press, 1999.

Boorstin, Daniel. *The Image: A Guide to Pseudo-Events in America*. New York: Atheneum, 1975.

Cassagneres, Ev. *The Spirit of Ryan*. Blue Ridge Summit, Pa.: Tab Books, 1982.

Cole, Wayne S. *Charles A. Lindbergh and the Battle Against American Intervention in World War II*. New York: Harcourt Brace Jovanovich, 1974.

Crouch, Tom D., ed. *Charles A. Lindbergh: An American Life*. Washington, D.C.: National Air and Space Museum, Smithsonian Institution, 1977.

Davies, R. E. G. *Charles Lindbergh: An Airman, His Aircraft, and his Great Flights*. McLean, Va.: Paladwr Press, 1997.

Davis, Kenneth S. *The Hero: Charles A. Lindbergh and the American Dream*. Garden City, N.Y.: Doubleday & Company, 1959.

Emme, Eugene M. *Aeronautics and Astronautics: An American Chronology of Science and Technology in the Exploration of Space, 1915–1960*. Washington, D.C.: National Aeronautics and Space Administration, 1961.

Fried, Albert. *FDR and His Enemies*. New York: Palgrave, 1999.

Gray, Susan M. *Charles A. Lindbergh and the American Dilemma: The Conflict of Technology and Human Values*. Bowling Green, Ohio: Bowling Green State University Popular Press, 1988.

Grierson, John. *I Remember Lindbergh*. New York: Harcourt Brace Jovanovich, 1977.

Hall, Donald A. *Technical Preparation of the Airplane "Spirit of St. Louis"*. Technical Note, National Advisory Committee for Aeronautics, No. 257. Reprinted in *Charles A. Lindbergh: An American Life*. Edited by Tom D. Crouch. Washington, D.C.: National Air and Space Museum, Smithsonian Institution, 1977, 83-93.

Hallion, Richard P. "Charles A. Lindbergh and Aviation Technology," in *Charles A. Lindbergh: An American Life*. Edited by Tom D. Crouch. Washington, D.C.: National Air and Space Museum, Smithsonian Institution, 1977, 39–48.

Hamlen, Joseph R. *Flight Fever*. Garden City, N.Y.: Doubleday & Company, 1971.

Herrmann, Dorothy. *Anne Morrow Lindbergh: A Gift for Life*. New York: Penguin Books, 1993.

Hessen, Robert, ed. *Berlin Alert: The Memoirs and Reports of Truman Smith*. Stanford, Calif.: Hoover Institution Press, Stanford University, 1984.

Hixson, Walter L. *Charles A. Lindbergh: Lone Eagle*. Library of American Biography. Edited by Oscar Handlin. New York: Harper Collins College Publishers, 1996.

Hoare, Robert J. *Wings Over the Atlantic.* Boston: Charles T. Branford, 1957.

Jablonski, Edward. *Atlantic Fever.* New York: The Macmillan Co., 1972.

Keyhoe, Donald E. *Flying With Lindbergh.* New York: G. P. Putnam's Sons, 1928.

Lardner, John. "The Lindbergh Legends." In *The Aspirin Age, 1919–1941.* Edited by Isabel Leighton. New York: Simon & Schuster, 1949, 190-213.

Lindbergh, Anne Morrow. *The Wave of the Future, A Confession of Faith.* New York: Harcourt, Brace and Company, 1940.

Lindbergh, Charles A. *Autobiography of Values.* Edited by William Jovanovich and Judith A. Schiff. New York: Harcourt Brace Jovanovich, 1976.

_____. *Of Flight and Life.* New York: Charles Scribner's Sons, 1948.

_____. *The Spirit of St. Louis.* New York: Charles Scribner's Sons, 1953.

_____. *"We": The Famous Flier's Own Story of His Life and Transatlantic Flight.* Foreword by Myron T. Herrick. New York: G. P. Putnam's Sons, 1927.

Lindbergh, Reeve. *Under A Wing: A Memoir.* New York: Delta, 1999.

Luckett, Perry D. *Charles A. Lindbergh: A Bio-Bibliography.* Westport, Conn.: Greenwood Press, 1986.

Milton, Joyce. *Loss of Eden: A Biography of Charles and Anne Morrow Lindbergh.* New York: HarperCollins Publishers, 1993.

Mosley, Leonard. *Lindbergh: A Biography.* Garden City, N.Y.: Doubleday & Company, 1976.

Nevin, David. *The Pathfinders.* Epic of Flight Series. Alexandria, Va.: Time-Life Books, 1980.

Ross, Walter S. *The Last Hero: Charles A. Lindbergh.* Revised edition. New York: Harper & Row, 1976.

Sherry, Michael S. *The Rise of American Air Power: The Creation of Armageddon.* New Haven, Conn.: Yale University Press, 1987.

Ward, John William. "The Meaning of Lindbergh's Flight." *In Studies in American Culture:Dominant Ideas and Images.* Edited by Joseph J. Kwiat and Mary C. Turpie. Minneapolis, Minn.: University of Minnesota Press, 1960, 27-40.

Wecter, Dixon. *The Hero in America: A Chronicle of Hero Worship.* Ann Arbor, Mich.: University of Michigan Press, 1963.

Wolfe, Tom. *The Right Stuff.* New York: Bantam Books, 1980.

Wright Aeronautical Corporation. *Wright Aviation Engines: Technical Features of the 1927 Production Model of the Wright Whirlwind 200-225 H.P. Nine Cylinder Air-Cooled Radial Engine.* Bulletin No. 21. Paterson, N.J.: Wright Aeronautical Corporation, 1927.

ARTICLES

Barrett, Howard. "Tom Rutledge—Engine Builder for Lindbergh." *The Flyer* 9 (February 1970): 4–5, 8–9.

Bonney, Walter T. "Spirit of St. Louis." *Pegasus* 26 (May 1957): 7-9.

"Companies Who Contributed to Colonel Lindbergh's New York-Paris Flight." *Aviation* 22 (June 20, 1927): 1,370.

Delear, Frank J. "Lindbergh's Flight . . . and an If or Two." *Bee Hive* 32 (Summer 1957): 28.

Goldsborough, Brice. "The Earth Inductor Compass." *Aero Digest* 10 (June 1927): 542-558.

Goldstein, Laurence. "Lindbergh in 1927: The Response of Poets to the Poem of Fact." *Prospects* 5 (1980): 293–313.

Hall, Donald A. "Technical Preparation of the Ryan New York-Paris Airplane." *Aero Digest* 11 (July 1927): 36, 38, 106.

"History of Development of the Wright Whirlwind." *The Slipstream* 8 (August 1927): 10.

Horsfall, Jessie E. "Lindbergh's Start for Paris." *Aero Digest* 10 (June 1927): 503–13.

"How Lindbergh Hit the Target." *The AC News* 2 (September 1927): 1.

Keyhoe, Donald E. "Seeing America with Lindbergh." *National Geographic* 53 (January 1928): 1–46.

Lindbergh Charles A. "My Flight to Paris." *Aero Digest* 10 (June 1927): 514–29.

Lindbergh, Charles A. "To Bogota and Back by Air." *National Geographic* 53 (May 1928): 529–601.

"Lindbergh 1927 New York to Paris Survival Equipment." *Journal of the American Aviation Historical Society* 242 (Spring 1979): 73–74.

"Lindbergh's Full Story of his Atlantic Flight by Himself." *Current History* 26 (July 1927): 506–610.

"Lindbergh's Wright Whirlwind a Result of Seven Years' Development." *Aviation* 22 (June 20, 1927): 1,358–59, 1,361.

McLaughlin, George F. "Ryan NY-P 'Spirit of St. Louis.'" *Aero Digest* 64 (May 1952): 26–40.

Miles, Russell H. "How the New York to Paris Plane Was Built." *Aviation* 22 (June 20, 1927): 1,352–53.

Morrow, Ed. "The Ed Morrow Story—Part 1." *Vintage Airplane* 13 (June 20, 1985): 20–24.

Reich, Leonard S. "From the *Spirit of St. Louis* to the SST: Charles Lindbergh, Technology, and Environment." *Technology and Culture* (April 1995): 351–93.

"Ryan Airlines, Inc., Reorganizing." *Aviation* 22 (March 14, 1927): 529.

"Ryan NY-P a Development of the Ryan M-2." *Aviation* 22 (June 20, 1927): 1,364, 1,366, 1,368.

"The *Spirit of St. Louis*: The Ryan Monoplane Described." *Flight* 19 (June 9, 1927): 376–79, 385.

Sudsbury, Elretta. "The Don Hall Story." *Naval Aviation News* 41 (September 1960): 12–15.

Titterington, Maurice M. "The Pioneer Earth Inductor Compass." *Aviation* 22 (June 20, 1927): 1,356–57, 1,400.

van der Linde, J. J. "How We Built Slim's 60-Day Wonder." *Air & Space Smithsonian* 2 (April/May 1987): 92–95.

"The Wright Whirlwind J-5C Engine." *Aero Digest* 10 (June 1927): 540–41.

UNPUBLISHED MANUSCRIPT

Kinney, Jeremy R. "The Propeller That Took Lindbergh Across: America's Development of the Metal Ground-Adjustable Pitch Propeller, 1917-1927." Paper presented at the 9th Biennial Meeting of the Conference of Historic Aviation Writers, St. Louis, Missouri, October 22–24, 1999.

INDEX

ACKNOWLEDGMENTS

The authors are grateful for the efforts of the following persons in helping to produce this work: Mark Avino; Ev Cassagneres, R. E. G. Davies; Tracy Drea; Phil Edwards; Trish Graboske; Kate Igoe; Allan Janus; Kristine Kaske; Melissa Keiser; Eric Long; Don Lopez; William Massa, Yale University; Ted Maxwell; Brian Nicklas; Dan Patterson; Natalie Rjedkin-Lee; Judith Schiff, Yale University; and Collette Williams.

PHOTOGRAPH CREDITS

Photograph credits include the negative number whenever possible. Photographs from the archives of the National Air and Space Museum, Smithsonian Institution, are identified below by NASM. Photographs credited to Yale University are from the Charles A. Lindbergh Collection, Sterling Memorial Library, Yale University.

FRONT COVER: (background) detail 89-21560 NASM, (foreground) detail 2001-6534 NASM. **BACK COVER**: detail A19864M NASM. **ENDPAPERS**: (front) detail 2001-4269 NASM, (back) detail 2001-4168 NASM.

PAGE 1: 2001-4269 NASM. **2**: detail (from p. 86), Yale University. **3**: A1598 NASM. **8–9**: A12783C ExxonMobil via NASM. **12–13**: A12720B ExxonMobil via NASM. **14**: A12720D NASM. **15**: 19864N NASM. **16**: 3199 Yale University. **17**: 76-15189 NASM. **20**: 85-12324 NASM. **23**: 92-3122 NASM. **25**: 78-12207 NASM. **27**: A49499B NASM. **28**: 2001-3225 Corbis via NASM. **29**: A31230C Ayer Company Publishers via NASM. **30**: A48597C NASM. **33**: 2001-2949 NASM. **34**: 2001-4322 NASM. **35**: (top) 2001-4323 NASM, (bottom) A47065E NASM. **36–37**: A4818D NASM. **38**: NASM. **39**: 2001-1352 NASM. **40**: 88-96 NASM. **42–43**: 71-1090 NASM. **44**: NASM. **45**: 2001-1842 NASM. **46**: 2001-3223 Honeywell via NASM. **47**: 2001-4168 NASM. **50**: 2001-1636 NASM. **52**: 2001-4159 NASM. **53**: 2001-4324 NASM. **54**: 94-8819 NASM. **57**: 89-21560 NASM **58**: 73-7365 NASM. **59**: 2001-4167 NASM. **60–61**: 77-2701 NASM. **62**: 3206 Yale University. **63**: A627A NASM. **64–65**: 80-9659 NASM. **67**: (top) 2001-4155 NASM, (bottom) 78-9329 NASM. **68**: 77-2700 *The New York Times* via NASM. **70**: 78-17771 NASM. **71**: A12720G ExxonMobil via NASM. **72–73**: 77-3240 NASM. **74**: (top) A12785L ExxonMobil via NASM, (bottom) A12583D ExxonMobil via NASM. **75**: 77-3106 NASM. **76–77**: A19864M NASM. **78**: 97-15222 NASM. **79**: A42064D NASM. **80**: A42064 NASM. **81**: A42065A NASM. **82**: 2001-4162 NASM. **84**: 3259 Yale University. **85**: 83-2469 *The New York Times* via NASM. **86**: Yale University. **89**: 3259 Yale University. **90**: 94-6292 NASM. **91**: 89-20586 NASM. **92**: 2001-4164 NASM. **93**: (top) 2001-4156 NASM, (bottom) 2001-4259 NASM. **97**: A45256E NASM. **99**: 3268 Yale University. **100**: Yale University. **101**: 3249 Yale University. **103**: 3279 Yale University. **106**: 79-10994 NASM. **111**: 3250 Yale University. **112**: Yale University. **113**: Yale University. **115**: Yale University. **117**: 3221 Yale University. **120**: A42065A NASM. **123**: 2001-4161 NASM. **124–25**: A746C NASM. **126**: A746 NASM. **127**: A742A NASM. **129**: 2001-6534 NASM. **134**: A45132 NASM. **144**: detail A48626C NASM.